# CHIANTI FAMILY COOKING

Giovanna Folonari Ruffino

# CHIANTI FAMILY COOKING

## Classic Recipes from the Heart of Tuscany

*Introduction by Michele Evans*

TIMES 🆃 BOOKS

RANDOM HOUSE

*To my children, Francesca, Giovanni, and Angelica*

## ACKNOWLEDGMENT

I am deeply indebted to my friend Michele Evans, the American food writer, who provided invaluable editorial assistance and the warm foreword to the English language edition of this book.

It came as no surprise to me that her sensitive understanding and passion for Italian food earned her the prestigious James Beard Foundation Award as co-author of the Best Italian Cookbook in 1997, *Gangivecchio's Kitchen*.

Copyright © 1999 by Casa Editrice Le Lettere

All rights reserved under International and Pan-American Copyright Conventions. Published in the United States by Times Books, a division of Random House, Inc., New York, and simultaneously in Canada by Random House of Canada Limited, Toronto.

This work was originally published in Italian in 1997 by Casa Editrice Le Lettere, Florence, Italy. Copyright © 1997 by Casa Editrice Le Lettere-Firenze.

Library of Congress Cataloging-in-Publication Data is available.

ISBN 0-8129-3138-6

Random House website address: www.randomhouse.com
Printed in Italy

98765432

First U.S. Edition

*Printer*: Vincenzo Bona S.r.l.-Torino
*Lithographed films*: Zincotecnica
*Graphic Designer*: Argoment-Firenze

*SPECIAL SALES*
Times Books are available at special discounts for bulk purchases for sales promotions or premiums. Special editions, including personalized covers, excerpts of existing books, and corporate imprints, can be created in large quantities for special needs. For more information, write to Special Markets, Times Books, 201 East 50th Street, New York, New York 10022, or call 800-800-3246.

# $C$ONTENTS

# *Foreword*

## Michele Evans

*New York*

Any mention of Tuscany releases a surge of associations drawn from a memory bank of many joyful journeys there. Unforgettable days spent contemplating the astonishing physical beauty of Tuscany's diverse landscape, its magnificent ancient culture and art, the pastoral tranquillity of the countryside, and the intense, constantly changing sunlight. The senses peak, recalling the intoxicating scent of pine trees, lavender-perfumed meadows, herb gardens, and rosemary, and olive-oil-basted meat roasting aromatically over wood burning embers. All thoughts spontaneously turn to Tuscany's extraordinary food. Surely anyone passionate about Tuscany must be passionate about its cuisine: noble, yet appealingly well balanced, probably the least complex of any region of Italy. Tuscan food is rustic, honest food, prepared with locally produced, seasonal quality ingredients like porcini mushrooms, black and white truffles, fine olive oils, superb vine-ripened produce, chestnuts, pine nuts, cheeses, and celebrated meats, wheat for world-class homemade pastas and breads, and, of course, superior wines. Like so many others, I am passionate about the region's food, but none are more passionate on the subject than the citizens of Tuscany.

One remarkable resident is Giovanna Folonari Ruffino, the author of this book, who has lived at Villa di Zano, near Greve in Chianti, in the heart of Chianti Classico, for thirty-five years. A wife and mother of three, Giovanna is a strikingly handsome, engaging woman with a luminous smile, a mischievous sense of humor, boundless energy, and a natural, sophisticated style. She has a tremendous talent for life. Her cooking skills have evolved from years of preparing family meals and producing beautiful dinner parties.

As a young bride, entertaining became an immediate fact of life, for Giovanna had become a member of the family which owns and produces the great Ruffino wines. In the culinary choreography of Giovanna Folonari Ruffino's kitchen, the steps may vary from meal to meal, but the wines always lead.

"Instead of selecting a good wine to serve with a meal, I had to do the opposite. I had to find good food to complement our fine Chianti wines. Of course, at first, I principally used the cherished family recipes handed down to me, but over the years, I also began collecting recipes of delicious dishes from friends living in other areas of Italy, from Puglia to Lombardy."

In 1985, to share her knowledge and genuine enthusiasm for food with others, she established a cooking school in the kitchen of her family's imposing eighteenth-century home, Villa di Zano. That required the transformation of the traditional Tuscan kitchen into an ultra-modern facility with gleaming professional equipment, vast work areas, and seating for twenty. An overhead angled mirror was installed so even the students in the last row could see every step and detail of preparation involved. Today, she continues teaching her classes, "Ruffino's Tuscan Experience," inspiring students from all over the world.

It was inevitable that Giovanna would write a cookbook. I, for one, am delighted she did, because this slim volume of one hundred of Giovanna Folonari Ruffino's beloved recipes, complemented by Guglielmo de Micheli's exquisite photographs, is a Tuscan culinary treasure, to be kept on the kitchen cookbook shelf, close to the stove. Rather than written as an encyclopedic volume of food fundamentals, it was lovingly assembled for home cooks who already have a basic knowledge of cooking. Her goal was to transport the dishes she teaches her students and serves on her own table in the Chianti countryside to your home.

Refreshingly, this unassuming collection of Giovanna's favorite recipes has no extraneous comments, instructions, or reminiscences. With genuine modesty, she insists she has no relevant advice to offer: only her recipes, along with the many dishes that she meticulously cooked and composed for the camera's lens. Giovanna's cookbook philosophy is that, after demonstrations and hands-on experience, photographs speak louder than words.
The typically elegant, authentic, straightforward Tuscan and Italian family recipes contained in this volume are incredibly easy to follow and they work. I know, because I've tasted many of the dishes in Giovanna's home and duplicated the aromas, flavors, and contrasting textures back in my own American kitchen with outstanding results.

Most of Giovanna's dishes are as light and delicious as the first meal she served to me on a late summer day this year. That meal began with thin crêpes filled with a radicchio-infused béchamel sauce, baked until golden on top. The main course was lean, slender scallops of veal with a delicate whipped horseradish cream sauce, served with sliced porcini mushrooms cooked briefly in a small amount of olive oil with a minced garlic clove and a shower of parsley. Dessert was Budino dei Medici, an ambrosial bread pudding made with brioche slices, golden raisins, and lemon zest, now a favorite of mine.

During that summer visit, I also remember standing with other friends and guests on the sprawling green lawn that surrounds Giovanna's newly renovated, spacious Tuscan stone house, a few hundred meters down the hill from Villa di Zano. Beyond the lawn and hedges of rosemary, lavender, broom, and oleander were acres of olive trees and endless rows of immaculately tended vineyards, old and new.

We picked the first ripe walnuts off the branches of the towering tree overhead; shelled, peeled, and nibbled their fresh nutty meat as an appetizer before a splendid luncheon outdoors. We feasted on a menu of seafood risotto, vitello tonnato, savory roasted red and yellow peppers, a crisp green salad, and Torta al Cioccolato, a light but flavorful, wickedly delicious chocolate tart, another new favorite in our home. After the tart, fresh figs, picked earlier in the day from a nearby tree, were placed on the table.

These are only a few of the memorable dishes from Giovanna Folonari Ruffino's extraordinary personal culinary legacy, which will bring the authentic aromas and flavors from her kitchen in Chianti in Tuscany to your own table.

# Introduction

Giovanna Folonari Ruffino

*Greve in Chianti*

As I write these words of introduction, it is only now that I realize, with deep emotion, gratitude to many people, and a certain disbelief that my recipes are actually being transformed from handwritten scribbles into a printed and photographed reality. You see, my beloved recipes have kept me occupied, preoccupied, thrilled, and amused for many years. It was twelve years ago that I began a cooking school, "Ruffino's Tuscan Experience," in our Villa di Zano, in the heart of the Chianti Classico hills near Greve in Chianti, in Tuscany. In these classes, I taught the family dishes that I knew and loved so well, marrying them with our fine wines. While I enjoyed this work tremendously back then, I never contemplated writing a book.

But after several years, when kind friends and my students kept asking, "Giovanna, why don't you write a cookbook?", I always answered that it seemed to me presumptuous; after all, I was not and I am not a professional cook. I was and I am simply an enthusiastic food lover, an aspiring artisan.

But my "Chianti Family Cookbook" began occupying my mind more and more, becoming a necessary part of each day: retesting my recipes, serving and tasting them until totally satisfied.

During this period, I finally came to understand that a pressing need existed within to preserve not only the family recipes handed down to me, but also the precious ones collected from friends from virtually every region of Italy, as well as the recipes I have created over the years. These are the dishes served on our table at home every day.

Ultimately, the one who forced me to make the decision to write the book was our good friend Giovanni Gentile, now my editor. One evening in his home, with some hesitation, I spoke to him about the idea of the book. He was immediately so enthusiastic that it scared me a little. He invited me to his office to discuss the matter seriously.

I came armed with my recipes, quite nervous, and I presented the concept that had been whirling around in my mind: a collection of one hundred recipes, suggestions for wines, with a lot of photographs. No long stories, explanations, or advice.

For me, photographs are (or should be) a crucial element in learning the art of cooking. Whenever I try a new recipe from a cookbook, magazine, or newspaper, the end result must appear exactly as it does in the picture. This accomplishment always gives me a sense of security in cooking. I wanted the recipes and the pictures in my book to be honest and to teach others.

When I stopped speaking, Giovanni told me to start cooking immediately, so the pictures could be taken, because everything had to be completed in five months. He had just introduced me to one of the terrifying aspects of publishing: deadlines.

And so began a culinary marathon, with the necessary stages. First, repeated trips for the food shopping and then a constant confusion of pots and pans, bowls, platters, molds, tablecloths, napkins, wineglasses, cutlery, and flowers; kitchen counters piled high with bunches of parsley, bouquets of basil, rosemary, and sage, heaps of garlic heads, onions, pine nuts, vegetables, cheeses, pastas, meat, fish, wine, bread, and olive oil. Then, cooking most of the dishes from antipasto to dessert, and doing whatever my talented and demanding photographer, Guglielmo de Micheli, required.

Guglielmo, whom I have known since he was born, set his studio up in the foyer of our home. He staged the area with lights, funny umbrellas, and strange photographic gadgets, all stationed around a table. Up on a small ladder, without a break, he shot dish after dish that Lina Verniani and I carefully prepared for him.

Yes, my Lina, my beloved Lina, my great, wise, devoted and cheerful inspiration. Without her, I confess, I would never have learned to love and enjoy cooking.

For two months, Guglielmo, Lina, and I worked harmoniously as a team. The pictures were born in a joyous atmosphere of laughter and gaiety, followed by huge tastings shared with our family and good friends.

The lights of our little studio were finally switched off, all the equipment removed. My house is now back to its quiet, reassuring tidiness and calm. All our work is in the capable hands of the graphic designer, the editor, and printer.

Of course, I'm waiting eagerly, so excited to hold the book in my hands. Sincerely I want to thank all of you who believed in my beloved recipes. Most of all, I hope that these recipes will bring great satisfaction and pleasure to my children and to all who try them.

# SUGGESTED WINES

FOR ANTIPASTO:

**Orvieto Classico Ruffino**

Bianco delle Cinque Terre

Galestro

Tocai del Piave

Franciacorta Bianco


FOR PHEASANT PÂTÉ:

**Nero del Tondo -** Pinot nero **Ruffino**

Grignolino del Monferrato

Bardolino Classico


FOR SEAFOOD:

**Cabreo la Pietra -** Chardonnay **Ruffino**

Vernaccia di S. Gimignano

Montecarlo Bianco

Sauvignon del Collio

Chardonnay Valdadige

# Antipasto and Seafood

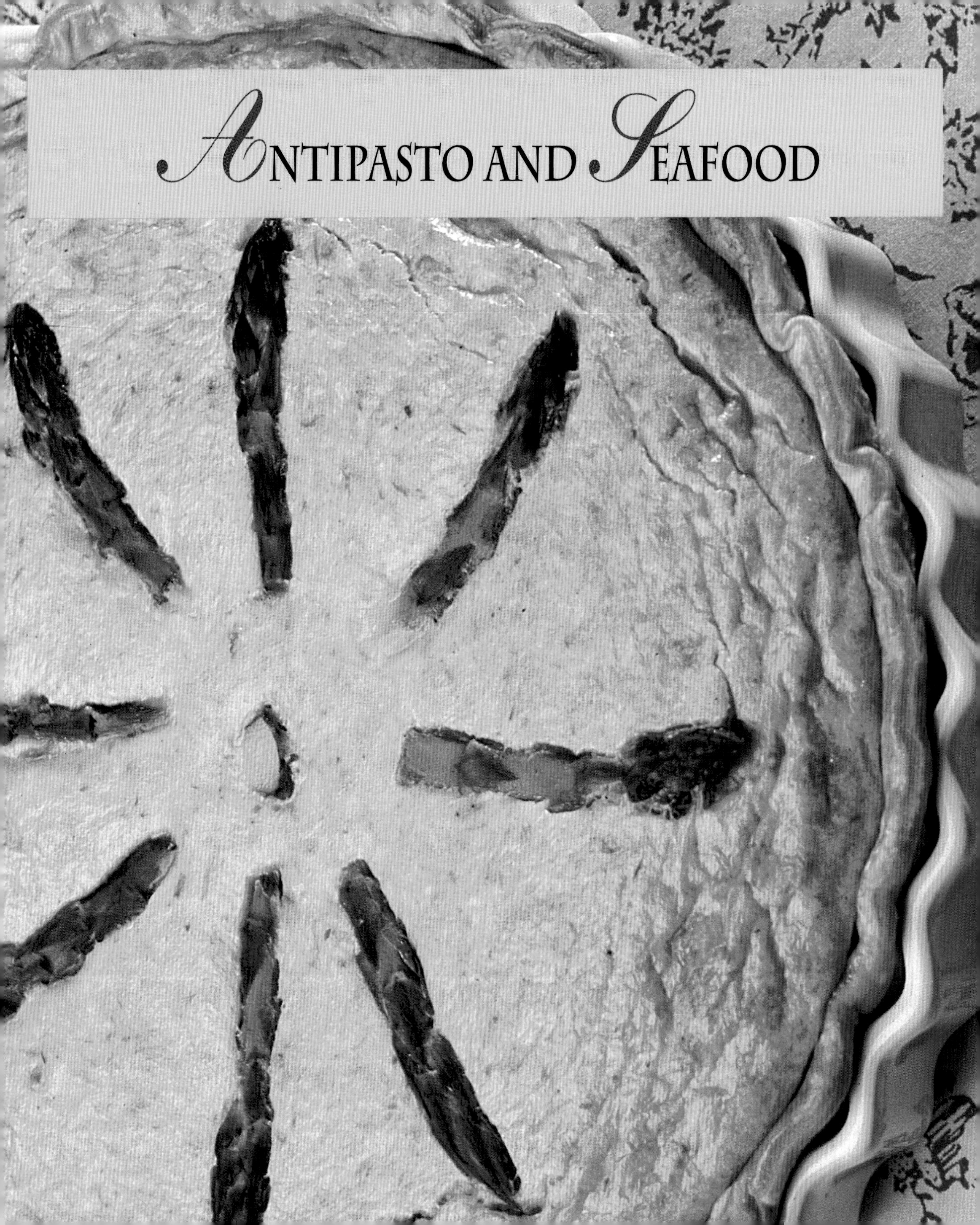

## INVOLTINI DI MELANZANA E PROSCIUTTO
### EGGPLANT ROLLS WITH HAM

Wash and dry the eggplants. Cut into thin slices lengthwise.

Dice the mozzarella.

Dust the eggplant slices with flour and fry in hot oil on both sides. Add more oil as needed. Drain on paper towels as cooked.

Preheat the oven to 375°F.

Cut sliced ham approximately the same size as the eggplant slices.

Place a slice of ham and a few dices of mozzarella on each eggplant slice and lightly salt. Roll up the eggplant and secure with a toothpick. Continue procedure until all eggplant slices are stuffed and rolled.

Grease a shallow baking dish with butter and place the eggplant rolls in it. Spoon equal amounts of tomato sauce over each roll and sprinkle with grated Parmesan cheese. Sprinkle with the melted butter.

Bake for 15 minutes in the oven.

*10 SERVINGS*

3 medium-sized eggplants

1/2 pound mozzarella

flour for dusting

extra-virgin olive oil for frying

7 ounces boiled ham, thinly sliced

salt

butter for greasing dish

4 tablespoons tomato sauce

3 tablespoons grated Parmesan cheese

2 tablespoons melted butter

## INSALATINA TIEPIDA DI PATATE CECI E BACCALÀ
### WARM SALAD OF POTATOES, CHICKPEAS, AND DRIED SALT COD

*6 SERVINGS*

1 1/2 pounds salt cod, soaked overnight
3 tablespoons extra-virgin olive oil
2 cloves garlic
6 small boiling or new potatoes
salt
2 cups cooked chickpeas
3 teaspoons chopped parsley
pepper

Wash, skin, and bone the salt cod and cut into small pieces.

Grease a shallow pan with 1 tablespoon oil and arrange the salt cod in it. Add the cloves of garlic, cover, hermetically sealing with foil. Steam for about 20 minutes over low heat.

Peel the potatoes and cut into slices. Season with a little salt and boil until tender, then drain.

Arrange the cooked potato slices on a hot serving dish. Crumble the salt cod on top and sprinkle with the chickpeas.

Process the cooking liquid of the fish (without the cloves of garlic), two tablespoons of extra-virgin olive oil, parsley, pepper, and a little salt in a blender for a few seconds.

Pour over the salad and serve lukewarm.

*6 SERVINGS*

2 large boneless and skinless
chicken breasts, boiled

2 ounces golden raisins

juice of 2 lemons

2 ounces extra-virgin olive oil

pinch of grated lemon zest

2 teaspoons chopped parsley

salt

a few drops of balsamic vinegar

2 heads red radicchio

# INSALATA DI POLLO E RADICCHIO
## CHICKEN SALAD AND RADICCHIO

Cut the chicken breasts into small cubes.

Soak the raisins in lukewarm water with a dash of lemon juice for 10 minutes. Drain.

Put the chicken cubes into a bowl to marinate with the raisins, remaining lemon juice, olive oil, grated lemon zest, and parsley. Lightly salt. Add balsamic vinegar to taste and mix well.

Let the mixture marinate for a few hours in the refrigerator.

Just before serving, cut the radicchio into thin strips and arrange on a serving dish. Spoon the chicken salad on top with the marinade.

*4 SERVINGS*

8 ounces ricotta

4 ounces plain yogurt

1/2 teaspoon Dijon mustard

3 tablespoons mixed fresh herbs
(parsley, marjoram, and thyme), chopped

1 spring onion, chopped

1 tablespoon extra-virgin olive oil

salt and pepper

2 ripe avocados

juice of 1/2 lemon

1 ripe tomato, peeled, seeded, and diced

## AVOCADO CON CREMA ALLE ERBE
### AVOCADO WITH FRESH HERB CREAM

Mix the ricotta with the yogurt, mustard, herbs, and onion in a bowl.
Dress with oil, salt, and pepper.

Peel the avocados, cut each in half, and remove the pits. Cut the avocados into thin
slices and sprinkle with lemon juice.

Spoon the ricotta sauce into the center of a round serving dish and arrange the slices
of avocado around it. Garnish with diced tomato.

## SFORMATO DI CARCIOFI
### ARTICHOKE TIMBALE

Preheat the oven to 375°F.

Clean the artichokes by removing the hard outer leaves, leaving only the tender inner hearts. Cut the hearts into thin slices.

Put the oil into a frying pan with the clove of garlic and cook until the garlic is golden. Add the artichokes and white wine and cook over low heat, adding salt, and pepper, until the artichokes are tender.

Stir in the flour, and cook for approximately 2 minutes; add the hot milk, mix well and cook for 5 minutes more. Remove the pan from the heat, add the eggs and the Parmesan cheese. Combine well.

Lightly grease a round 4-cup mold and sprinkle with bread crumbs. Pour the artichoke mixture into the mold, cover with foil. Set the mold in a pan with hot water coming halfway up the sides of the mold, like a bain-marie. Cook in the oven for approximately 20 minutes.

Remove from oven and from bain-marie. Let it rest for a few minutes. Unmold and serve with cheese sauce (see following recipe).

*6 SERVINGS*

10 medium-sized artichokes
2 tablespoons extra-virgin olive oil
1 clove garlic
splash of dry white wine
salt and pepper
1/2 cup all-purpose flour
2 cups milk
2 large eggs
2 tablespoons grated Parmesan cheese
4 ounces unsalted butter
1 ounce dried bread crumbs

## CREMA DI FORMAGGIO
### CHEESE SAUCE

Melt the butter in a small casserole. Add the flour and cook for one minute, stirring constantly.

Little by little, add boiling milk, always stirring.

Whisk in the cheeses and cook until smooth and creamy, stirring constantly. Season with salt and pepper.

*6 SERVINGS*

1 ounce unsalted butter
1 1/2 tablespoons all-purpose flour
2 cups boiling milk
1 1/2 ounces Emmenthal
2 ounces mascarpone
1 ounce grated Parmesan cheese
salt and pepper

**8 SERVINGS**

FOR THE PASTRY:

2 cups all-purpose flour

1 large egg

salt and pepper

1 tablespoon extra-virgin olive oil

FOR THE FILLING:

2 pounds small leeks

2 tablespoons olive oil

salt and pepper

4 large eggs

3 ounces smoked pancetta or bacon, chopped fine

1 1/4 cups heavy cream

## TORTINA AI PORRI
### LEEK PIE

To make the pastry:
Mix the ingredients well for a few minutes until a soft, elastic ball is obtained. Put in the refrigerator covered in plastic wrap.

Preheat the oven to 350°F.

Wash the leeks and cut them into thin circles. Sauté in a pan with the olive oil over medium heat. Season to taste with salt and pepper. Cover with a lid as soon as they are golden, in order to soften them completely.

Remove from heat and let cool before mixing with the eggs, bacon, and cream. Add salt to taste.

Roll out the pastry and fit into an 8- to 9-inch round tart pan.

Pour the mixture into the pan. Cook in the oven about 45 minutes or until the top is golden. Serve hot.

# BUDINO AL PARMIGIANO REGGIANO
PARMESAN CHEESE PUDDING

Preheat the oven to 375°F.

Beat the eggs and add the sifted flour, grated Parmesan cheese, milk, and cream. Combine well. Season with salt and pepper.

Grease a pudding pan or 4 individual molds. Pour in the mixture. Set the mold (or individual molds) into a pan with hot water coming halfway up the sides of the mold, like a bain-marie. Bake in the oven for about 30 minutes or until the pudding is firm to the touch.

Remove from oven and from bain-marie.

Invert onto a serving dish (or individual serving plates), unmold, and serve hot.

You can serve the pudding with porcini mushrooms, finely sliced and sautéed in olive oil with 1 chopped garlic clove for 5 to 6 minutes.

*4 SERVINGS*

4 large eggs
3 tablespoons sifted all-purpose flour
7 ounces grated Parmesan cheese
3/4 cup milk
3/4 cup heavy cream
salt and pepper
butter for greasing pan

*8 SERVINGS*

8 individual tart pans

FOR THE DOUGH:
2 cups all-purpose flour
1 cup unsalted butter
1 large egg, beaten
pinch of salt

FOR THE FILLING:
3/4 cup heavy cream
2 large eggs
6 1/2 ounces Gorgonzola
grated nutmeg
pepper
1 1/2 pounds pears
1 ounce grated Emmenthal

# TORTINO SALATO ALLE PERE
## SALTED PEAR TARTS

Prepare the dough:
Place the flour and butter, cut into pieces, in a large bowl. Incorporate beaten egg and a pinch of salt and mix together with pastry blender until coarsecrumb consistency. Knead the dough several times and form into a ball. Cover with plastic wrap and refrigerate 2 hours.

Preheat the oven to 400°F.

Prepare the filling:
Put the cream, eggs, Gorgonzola, pinch of grated nutmeg, and pepper into a blender. Process until well combined.

Roll out dough on a floured surface. Line individual tart pans. Prick dough on bottom of each with a fork.

Pour the Gorgonzola cream into each tart in equal amounts.

Peel and core the pears. Cut them into thin slices. Arrange decoratively over the filling in equal amounts.

Sprinkle with grated Emmenthal. Place the tarts on a baking sheet and cook in the oven for 30 minutes.

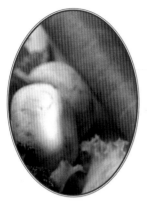

## MOSAICO DI VERDURA
### VEGETABLE MOSAIC

Preheat the oven to 300° F.

Cut the carrots and zucchini into thin 1 1/2-inch-long strips. Cut the mushrooms into thin slices.

Cook the carrots with 1 ounce butter, 1/2 cup of water, 2 pinches of salt, and sugar in a saucepan over medium heat until all the liquid has evaporated.

In another saucepan, stew the zucchini with the remaining butter, 1 clove of garlic, and a finely chopped sprig of thyme (using just the leaves). Cook 10 minutes.

Meanwhile, cook the mushrooms over high heat in a frying pan with 1 tablespoon of oil and 2 cloves of garlic. Season with salt and pepper and cook 5 to 6 minutes. Add the chopped parsley. Cool all the vegetables on paper towels.

Butter a rectangular nonstick 11- to 12-inch by 4- to 4 1/2-inch loaf pan.

Beat the eggs and cream in a bowl with salt and pepper. Pour a third of this mixture into the loaf pan. Add the zucchini, mushrooms, and carrots in layers lengthwise forming a colorful pattern, with a small quantity of egg mixture between each layer. Cover the top with egg-cream mixture.

Cover the pan with foil and set into a pan with hot water coming halfway up the sides of the pan, like a bain-marie. Cook in the oven for 60 minutes or until firm to the touch. Remove from oven. Let cool in the baking pan for 2 hours at room temperature. Cool in the refrigerator for 2 more hours. Unmold, slice, and serve with a salad.

*10 TO 12 SERVINGS*

12 ounces peeled carrots

12 ounces zucchini

12 ounces mushrooms

2 ounces unsalted butter

1/2 cup water

salt and pepper

1 teaspoon sugar

3 cloves garlic

sprig of fresh thyme

3 tablespoons extra-virgin olive oil

2 tablespoons chopped parsley

butter for greasing pan

5 large eggs

12 ounces heavy cream

## TORTA DI ASPARAGI
### ASPARAGUS TART

Preheat the oven to 350° F.

Wash the asparagus, remove the stalk ends and cook in boiling salted water for 7 to 8 minutes. Drain the asparagus. Cut off the tips and reserve them. Coarsely chop the stalks.

Put the coarsely chopped asparagus stalks, eggs, cheeses, and cream into a food processor. Process until smooth. Season with salt and pepper.

Line a 9-inch round cake pan with the puff pastry. Pour in the filling and decorate the top with the asparagus tips. Bring the edges of the dough up a little over the asparagus tips and brush with the beaten egg yolk.

Cook in the oven for about 1 hour.

*12 SERVINGS*

2 pounds asparagus

3 eggs

4 ounces Gorgonzola

2 ounces grated Parmesan cheese

1/2 pound Certosa (or other soft cheese, such as cream cheese)

1/2 cup heavy cream

salt and pepper

1/2 pound puff pastry, thawed

1 egg yolk for brushing pastry

# PÂTÉ DI FAGIANO
### PHEASANT PÂTÉ

Preheat the oven to 375° F.

To prepare the pheasant:
Wash and dry the pheasant. Coarsely chop half of pancetta together with the sage leaves and stuff the pheasant.

Line the breast with the remaining slices of pancetta and truss the pheasant. Secure the pancetta in place with kitchen string.

Place pheasant in a roasting pan and brush with olive oil. Season well with salt and pepper.

Cook in the oven for about 1/2 hour, turning from time to time.

Sprinkle the pheasant with the dry white wine and cook for another 20 minutes, covered with foil to keep it moist.

Remove from oven and let cool. Remove the skin and bones. Mince the meat and pancetta very fine.

Place the minced meat into a bowl. Add the mascarpone and mix well. Add the Marsala wine and, at the end, the whipped cream. Season with salt and pepper.

Line a rectangular mold measuring 10 to 11 inches by 4 inches with plastic wrap. Turn in the mixture and press it down gently. Cover with plastic wrap and refrigerate overnight.

Just before serving, unmold the pâté, remove the plastic wrap, and slice it with the moistened blade of a knife.

*8 SERVINGS*

1 pheasant (about 3 pounds)
3 1/2 ounces smoked pancetta, thinly sliced
4 fresh sage leaves
3 tablespoons extra-virgin olive oil
salt and pepper
1/2 cup dry white wine
10 ounces mascarpone
2 tablespoons Marsala wine
2 tablespoons whipped cream

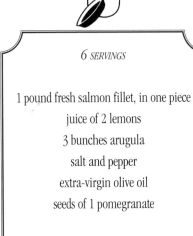

*6 SERVINGS*

1 pound fresh salmon fillet, in one piece

juice of 2 lemons

3 bunches arugula

salt and pepper

extra-virgin olive oil

seeds of 1 pomegranate

## CARPACCIO DI SALMONE
## CON RUCOLA E MELOGRANO
### SALMON CARPACCIO WITH ARUGULA AND POMEGRANATE SEEDS

Remove the skin and the bones from the salmon.

Freeze the fish for 2 hours.

Cut the partially frozen salmon into very thin slices, accomplished best by electric slicing machine.

Place the slices on a large platter and completely cover with lemon juice. Refrigerate for 1 hour.

Cut the arugula into thin strips. Arrange it into a bed on a serving dish.

Drain the lemon juice from salmon and place the slices over the arugula.

Season with salt, pepper, and olive oil and garnish with the pomegranate seeds.

*6 SERVINGS*

1 1/2 pounds small cuttlefish

2 eggs

2 tablespoons dried bread crumbs

3 tablespoons grated Parmesan cheese

1/2 clove garlic, minced; plus 1 whole clove

1 tablespoon finely chopped parsley

2 tablespoons milk

salt and pepper

1 tablespoon extra-virgin olive oil

2 tablespoons dry white wine

# TOTANI RIPIENI
## STUFFED CUTTLEFISH

Clean each cuttlefish well, leaving the sac in one piece and separating the tentacles. Wash under running water.

Mix the eggs, bread crumbs, Parmesan cheese, minced garlic, parsley (reserving 1 teaspoon), milk, salt, and pepper together in a bowl.

Grease a baking pan with 1/2 tablespoon of olive oil. Add the whole garlic clove.

With a teaspoon, fill the cuttlefish sacs half full with bread crumb and Parmesan mixture, and add cuttlefish tentacles at ends to close.

Lay the cuttlefish side by side in the pan and sprinkle with the remaining parsley, olive oil, and white wine. Lightly season with salt.

Cover with foil and cook in a preheated oven to 350°F for 20 minutes.

*6 SERVINGS*

1 1/2 pounds fresh shrimp,
shelled and deveined

all-purpose flour for dusting

salt

2 tablespoons extra-virgin olive oil

1 clove garlic

2 tablespoons fresh chopped parsley

2 tablespoons fresh chopped basil

1/4 cup dry white wine

2 ripe medium-sized fresh tomatoes

pepper

# SCAMPI ALLA PESCATORA
## FISHERMAN-STYLE SHRIMP

Lightly dust the shrimp with flour and season with salt.

Heat the oil in a skillet with the garlic. Add the shrimp and sauté for 2 minutes. Add the chopped parsley and basil and wine.

Peel, seed, and chop the tomatoes.

When the wine has completely evaporated, add the tomatoes and season with pepper. Stir briefly and serve very hot.

## TORTINI DI ALICI AL TIMO
### ANCHOVY PUDDINGS WITH THYME

**6 SERVINGS**

2 pounds fresh anchovies

7 ounces stale bread, grated

a few sprigs each fresh chopped basil, parsley, and thyme

1 ounce grated Pecorino or Parmesan cheese

salt and pepper

1/2 cup extra-virgin olive oil

Preheat the oven to 400° F.

Bone and clean the anchovies carefully. Wash, drain well, and pat dry with paper towels.

Combine the bread with the chopped herbs and cheese. Season with salt and pepper.

Grease 6 individual molds with olive oil and dust with the bread crumb mixture.

Place a first layer of anchovies into the mold, then a little of the bread crumb mixture, and sprinkle with olive oil. Continue with other layers and end by sprinkling the top lightly with olive oil.

Cook in the oven for about 20 minutes.

Unmold and serve hot.

## POLIPI ALLA LUCIANA
### NEAPOLITAN OCTOPUS

Wash the octopuses well and remove the entrails, eyes, and beak from each.

Put octopuses and remaining ingredients into a pot, cover with a lid, and put a weight on it.

Place the pot over a very low heat and cook about 1 1/2 hours. Don't open lid during cooking time. After cooking, let it rest for at least 20 minutes.

When you open the pot, you will see that the octopuses have turned a beautiful reddish-chrysanthemum color, and are very tender and floating in an exquisite broth.

Remove the octopuses from the pot, remove and discard the skin. Cut the octopuses into small pieces.

Place a small portion over fried polenta croutons and dress with a little of the broth.

*6 SERVINGS*

2 pounds medium-sized octopuses

1 cup extra-virgin olive oil

5 ripe tomatoes, peeled and coarsely chopped

3 cloves garlic

1/2 medium-sized white onion

1 celery stalk

handful of parsley

salt and pepper

## MOSCARDINI IN INSALATA
### BABY OCTOPUS SALAD

Cook the baby octopuses in boiling, salted water until tender when pierced with a fork. Drain and place in a glass bowl. Add the garlic, olive oil, vinegar, and salt and pepper to taste. Mix well and refrigerate for a few hours.

Peel the potatoes. Cube and cook them in boiling salted water until tender. Drain and cool.

Peel, seed, and cube the tomatoes.

Place the potatoes and tomatoes on a large serving dish. Dress with the marinade of the baby octopuses, discarding the garlic cloves. Arrange the octopuses on top.

Sprinkle with chopped parsley and refrigerate until served.

*8 SERVINGS*

2 pounds fresh baby octopuses

salt

3 cloves garlic

1/4 cup extra-virgin olive oil

2 tablespoons white wine vinegar

pepper

6 medium-sized boiling potatoes

3 medium-sized ripe tomatoes

chopped fresh parsley

## SEPPIE CON CARCIOFI
### SQUID WITH ARTICHOKES

**6 SERVINGS**

2 pounds squid

4 to 5 medium-sized artichokes

juice of 1/2 lemon

2 tablespoons extra-virgin olive oil

1 small onion, thinly sliced

1 clove garlic

1/2 cup dry white wine

salt and pepper

2 teaspoons chopped parsley

Clean the squid, removing the bones, ink sacs, eyes, and the beak inside each tentacle. Wash well under cool running water. Flatten the squid sacs well with a mallet on a chopping board. Cut the sacs into strips and tentacles into two sections.

Clean the artichokes by peeling away and eliminating the tough outer leaves and center. Cut the hearts into thin slices. Put into a bowl covered with water and the lemon juice.

Heat the oil with the onion and the garlic clove in a frying pan and cook over a low heat for 2 to 3 minutes. Add the squid and sauté for another 3 minutes. Sprinkle with white wine. Let the wine evaporate and cook covered for 15 minutes. Add the artichokes and season with salt and pepper. Lower the heat and cover. Let cook for another 30 minutes. Make sure there is always enough cooking juice so the dish does not burn; add a little hot water or vegetable broth if needed.

After about 45 minutes, remove the lid, raise the heat and let the mixture cook uncovered until the juice has reduced, about 10 minutes.

Add the chopped parsley, stir, and serve immediately.

## FILETTI DI SOGLIOLA ALLO YOGURT
### FILLET OF SOLE WITH YOGURT

Preheat the oven to 350° F.

Chop the onion, add thyme and parsley and mix with the olive oil. Cover the fillets with equal amounts of this mixture. Roll up each fillet gently.

Place the fillets in a greased shallow baking dish, upright, side by side, touching each other, in rows. Season with salt and pepper. Mix yogurt with the cream and pour over the fish.

Cook in the oven for 20 minutes.

Serve hot.

*8 SERVINGS*

1 small onion

1 tablespoon chopped fresh thyme

1 tablespoon chopped fresh parsley

2 tablespoons extra-virgin olive oil

16 small sole fillets

butter for greasing the pan

salt and pepper

1/2 cup plain yogurt

3/4 cup heavy cream

## SCALOPPA DI BRANZINO AL VINO BIANCO CON ACCIUGHE E CAPPERI
### SEA BASS SCALLOPS IN WHITE WINE WITH ANCHOVIES AND CAPERS

*4 SERVINGS*

2 medium-sized tomatoes

1 tablespoon extra-virgin olive oil

1 clove garlic

6 anchovy fillets, finely chopped

1 tablespoon capers

1/4 cup dry white wine

1 teaspoon finely chopped parsley

salt and pepper

1 pound sea bass fillet, cut into thin scallops

extra oil for cooking fish

Peel and seed the tomatoes and cut them into small cubes.

To prepare the sauce, lightly sauté the tomatoes in a frying pan with the oil and garlic, anchovies, and capers for 5 minutes. Add the wine and parsley. Cook another 5 minutes.

Meantime, sprinkle a little salt and pepper over the fish and cook in a large nonstick frying pan with a few drops of olive oil.

Arrange the scallops in 4 warmed dinner plates. Spoon equal amounts of the sauce over each serving, and serve immediately.

*8 TO 10 SERVINGS*

2 pounds salt cod, soaked overnight

all-purpose flour for dusting

4 tablespoons extra-virgin olive oil

pepper

grated nutmeg

1 ounce grated Parmesan cheese

1 small onion, finely chopped

1 clove garlic, chopped

6 anchovy fillets, chopped

1 tablespoon chopped parsley

1/4 cup dry white wine

1 1/4 cups milk

## BACCALÀ ALLA VICENTINA
### VICENZA'S CODFISH

Clean and skin the codfish, dry it well on paper towels, and cut it into 1 by 1 1/2-inch rectangular-shaped pieces. Dust with flour and arrange in one layer on a shallow baking pan lightly greased with 1 tablespoon olive oil. Season with pepper, grated nutmeg, and Parmesan cheese.

Lightly brown the onion and garlic in a small saucepan in the remaining oil over low heat. Add the anchovies and the parsley. Cook for 4 to 5 minutes. Add the wine and cook for 3 minutes.

Pour the mixture evenly over the codfish.

Preheat the oven to 375° F.

Just before putting the baking pan into the oven, heat the milk to almost boiling and pour it over the codfish. Cook, covered with foil, for about 25 to 30 minutes. Uncover for the last 5 minutes.

Serve very hot.

# SUGGESTED WINES

FOR PASTA AND CRÊPES:

**FONTE AL SOLE RUFFINO**

CHIANTI COLLI FIORENTINI

ROSSO DI MONTEPULCIANO

VALPOLICELLA

FOR SEAFOOD PASTA:

**LIBAIO** CHARDONNAY **RUFFINO**

PINOT GRIGIO DEI COLLI ORIENTALI DEL FRIULI

VERMENTINO LIGURE

FIANO DI AVELLINO

SOAVE CLASSICO

FOR RISOTTO:

**AZIANO** CHIANTI CLASSICO **RUFFINO**

LAGREIN TRENTINO

FOR SOUP:

DOLCETTO D'ASTI

MARZEMINO TRENTINO

ROSSO DI MONTALCINO

# PASTA AND FIRST-COURSE DISHES

*6 SERVINGS*

1 pound broccoli

salt

1/4 cup extra-virgin olive oil

3 cloves garlic

6 anchovy fillets

1 chili pepper, seeded and chopped

1 pound orecchiette

# ORECCHIETTE AI BROCCOLI
## ORECCHIETTE WITH BROCCOLI

Wash the broccoli and cut away the toughest part of the stalks.

Boil in 4 quarts of lightly salted water. Remove the broccoli with a slotted spoon and reserve the cooking water. Let cool, then cut into bite-sized pieces.

Put the oil, garlic, anchovies, and chili pepper into a frying pan and gently brown. Discard the cloves of garlic and pepper. Add the broccoli and simmer for a few minutes.

Cook the pasta in the boiling water the broccoli cooked in. Drain and turn it into the skillet with the broccoli sauce. Toss well and cook for a couple of minutes over medium heat.

Transfer to a serving bowl and serve at once.

## PENNETTE RUCOLA E SALSICCIA
### PENNETTE WITH ARUGULA AND SAUSAGE

*6 SERVINGS*

3 fresh Italian sweet sausages

3 tablespoons extra-virgin olive oil

3 bunches of arugula, cut into thin strips

3 medium-sized ripe tomatoes,
peeled, seeded, and diced

salt and pepper

1 teaspoon butter

1 teaspoon all-purpose flour

1 pound pennette or penne

grated Parmesan cheese

Remove casings from sausages.

Heat the oil in a large frying pan and add the sausage meat. Cook over medium heat for 2 to 3 minutes or until pink color is gone. Add the arugula and simmer for 2 minutes. Add the tomatoes. Season with salt and pepper. Cook for 2 more minutes.

Work the butter together with the flour and stir into the pan. Simmer, stirring often, until the sauce has thickened slightly.

In a large pot bring 4 quarts of salted water to a rolling boil, add the pasta and cook al dente, stirring often. Drain the pasta and return it to the pot. Immediately add the sauce and cook over low heat for 2 minutes, tossing frequently.

Serve immediately and pass the Parmesan cheese.

## PENNE ALLA PUTTANESCA
### PENNE PUTTANESCA

Coarsely chop the tomatoes.

Put the tomatoes, oil, garlic, capers, oregano, black olives, chili pepper, and the anchovies into a large frying pan.

Over a fairly high heat, cook the sauce, stirring frequently, for about 15 minutes. At the end of cooking, add the parsley and a pinch of pepper. Remove from heat.

In a pot, bring 4 quarts of water to a boil. Add 1 1/2 tablespoons salt. Cook the pasta al dente. Drain and put into the frying pan with the sauce. Sauté briefly on a high heat for a couple of minutes, tossing well.

Serve very hot.

*6 SERVINGS*

1 pound canned Italian plum tomatoes

1/2 cup extra-virgin olive oil

2 cloves garlic

1 tablespoon capers

1 teaspoon dried oregano

3 ounces pitted black olives, chopped

1 chili pepper, chopped

6 anchovy fillets, chopped

2 teaspoons chopped parsley

pepper and salt

1 1/2 pounds penne

## LINGUINE CON LE SEPPIE AL NERO
### LINGUINE WITH SQUID

*4 SERVINGS*

10 ounces squid, with ink sacs

1/4 cup extra-virgin olive oil

2 garlic cloves

salt and pepper

1/4 cup dry white wine

2 anchovy fillets

10 ounces canned Italian plum tomatoes

1 tablespoon chopped parsley

1 pound linguine

Clean the squid by removing the interior bone, skin, and innards, reserving the ink sacs. Cut the squid into strips.

Heat the oil and garlic in a nonstick frying pan. When hot, add the squid, season with salt and pepper and sauté for 5 minutes, stirring well. Add the wine and let evaporate for 3 to 4 minutes.

In a small pan with a little heated oil, cook the anchovies until almost dissolved and immediately add to the squid.

Pass the tomatoes through a sieve and add to the squid. Cook over a low heat for 30 minutes, stirring occasionally.

During the last minutes of cooking, puncture the ink sacs and add the ink to the pan to obtain the characteristic black color. Sprinkle with chopped parsley and remove from heat.

Cook the linguine al dente in 4 quarts of boiling, salted water.

Drain the pasta and pour it into the frying pan with squid sauce and simmer for 1 minute, tossing well.

## MACCHERONI ALL'AFFUMICATA
### MACARONI WITH SMOKED MOZZARELLA SAUCE

Dice the ham. Remove the outer skin of the mozzarella and cut it into thin slices.

In a small skillet, heat 1 ounces of the butter with the ham and the sage leaves. Cook gently for 3 to 4 minutes.

Put the cream in a little casserole with the mozzarella and 2 tablespoons of Parmesan cheese and cook over very low heat until the cheese has melted. Take off the heat and season with pepper.

While you prepare the cheese cream, bring 4 quarts of water to a boil in a big pot; add 1 1/2 tablespoons of salt. Stir in the pasta and cook al dente. Drain and return the pasta to the pot. Dress with the ham and the remaining butter. Cook over a low heat for a few seconds, mixing well.

Take off the heat, and stir in the cheese sauce. Transfer to a shallow, greased baking dish and dust the top with the remaining tablespoon of Parmesan cheese mixed with the bread crumbs.

Cook in a preheated 375° F oven for about 15 minutes to brown top slightly.

*6 SERVINGS*

5 ounces smoked ham, cut into thick slices

5 ounces smoked mozzarella

2 ounces unsalted butter,
plus extra for greasing pan

4 fresh sage leaves, chopped

1 cup heavy cream

3 tablespoons grated Parmesan cheese

pepper and salt

1 pound macaroni

2 tablespoons dried bread crumbs

# MAFALDINE AL PESTO CON PATATE E FAGIOLINI
## MAFALDINE AL PESTO WITH POTATOES AND GREEN BEANS

To make the pesto sauce:

Put the garlic, 2 tablespoons of oil, one cup of basil leaves, and 1 tablespoon of pine nuts into a food processor or blender and start processing, adding olive oil, little by little, until a creamy consistency is reached. Now add the remaining basil, Parmesan cheese, pine nuts, salt and pepper, and more oil, if needed, and process. The sauce must be quite thick. Set aside.

Peel the potatoes and cut them into small cubes.

Trim off ends of the green beans, and cut them in half.

Heat 4 quarts of water in a large pot. When the water starts boiling, add 1 1/2 tablespoons of salt and the green beans. After 4 to 5 minutes, add the potatoes.

When the vegetables are nearly cooked, add the pasta and cook al dente.

Drain the pasta and the vegetables, reserving a cup of the boiling water. Pour the mafaldine or fettuccine into a bowl. Dress with the pesto sauce and gently toss. Add a little of the boiling water and toss again.

*6 SERVINGS*

FOR THE PESTO SAUCE:
1/2 clove garlic, minced
extra-virgin olive oil
2 cups fresh basil leaves
3 tablespoons pine nuts
1/4 cup grated Parmesan cheese
salt and pepper

3 medium-sized boiling potatoes
1/2 pound green beans
salt
1 pound mafaldine or fettuccine

## SPAGHETTI CON BOTTARGA E RUCOLA
### SPAGHETTI WITH MULLET ROE AND ARUGULA

Place the olives in a bowl with the olive oil and basil leaves and let marinate for 1 hour.

Cut the bottarga into very thin slices and then crumble it. Cut the arugula into thin strips. Combine the bottarga and arugula in a serving bowl.

Process the olives, 1/6 cup oil, and basil in a blender and pour on top of the bottarga and arugula.

Bring 4 quarts of water to a boil. Stir in 1 1/2 tablespoons of salt. Add the spaghetti and cook al dente.

Drain and turn into the serving bowl. Dress with the remaining olive oil. Toss well and serve hot.

* Bottarga, dried pressed mullet eggs, can be found in specialty food shops.

*4 SERVINGS*

1 ounce pitted black olives

1/3 cup extra-virgin olive oil

10 leaves fresh basil

2 ounces bottarga *

2 cups fresh arugula

salt

1 pound spaghetti

# SPAGHETTI IN SALSA DI CIPOLLE
## SPAGHETTI WITH ONION SAUCE

*4 SERVINGS*

2 medium-sized white onions
1/4 cup extra-virgin olive oil
salt and pepper
4 anchovy fillets, chopped
1 pound spaghetti
grated Parmesan cheese

Slice the onions very thin.

Heat half of the olive oil in a large saucepan. Add the onions and 2 tablespoons of hot water, a pinch of salt and pepper, and cook over low heat, covered, for about 15 minutes.

Add the anchovies and cook for another 5 minutes. Add the remaining olive oil; remove from heat and keep warm.

Bring 4 quarts of water to a boil. Stir in 1 1/2 tablespoons of salt. Add the spaghetti and cook al dente.

Drain and put into a warmed serving bowl. Dress with the onion sauce, tossing it well.

Serve with grated Parmesan cheese.

## PENNE AGLI SPINACI E GORGONZOLA
### PENNE WITH SPINACH AND GORGONZOLA

*6 SERVINGS*

salt

1 pound frozen chopped spinach, thawed

1 pound penne

1/2 pound Gorgonzola

2 ounces mascarpone

1 ounce grated Parmesan cheese

pepper

Bring 4 quarts of water to a boil. When boiling, season with 1 1/2 tablespoons of salt, and then add the spinach. Cover the pot and let the water come to a boil again. Add the pasta, and let cook al dente. Stir often.

Meantime, put the Gorgonzola, cut into little pieces, mascarpone, and the Parmesan cheese into a heatproof dish in which you will serve the pasta. Work the cheeses together well with a fork. Season with pepper.

When the pasta is done, drain it with the spinach well, reserving 1 cup of the boiling water. Pour the pasta and spinach into the bowl with the cheeses, toss well, and put over the heat for a couple of minutes, tossing well. If too thick, add a small quantity of the reserved pasta water. Serve hot.

## STRANGOLAPRETI
### GNOCCHI WITH SPINACH AND RICOTTA

Melt the butter in a frying pan over medium heat. Squeeze the water out of the boiled spinach and finely chop.

Add the spinach to the pan and cook for 5 minutes, stirring frequently. Let cool.

Put the spinach into a bowl. Add the ricotta, flour, Parmesan, bread crumbs, and eggs. Mix the ingredients well. Add salt and pepper and season with grated nutmeg to taste. Place the mixture in the refrigerator for at least half an hour.

Remove the mixture from the refrigerator and roll it into little balls. Cook them in a large pot with plenty of salted boiling water for 4 to 5 minutes.

Remove the balls from the water with a skimmer. Drain them well and place in an ovenproof dish. Dot with melted butter and sage.

Before serving, sprinkle the top with some Parmesan cheese and, if desired, place the dish under a hot broiler a few minutes to lightly brown.

*8 TO 10 SERVINGS*

2 ounces unsalted butter

2 pounds boiled fresh spinach

1 pound ricotta

5 ounces sifted all-purpose flour

5 ounces grated Parmesan cheese

2 tablespoons dried bread crumbs

3 egg yolks plus 1 whole large egg

salt and pepper

nutmeg

To DRESS:

1 ounce unsalted butter, melted with 4 sage leaves

2 tablespoons grated Parmesan cheese

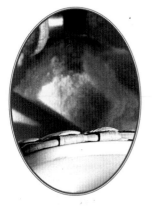

# ROTOLINI DI SPINACI E RICOTTA
## CRÊPES WITH SPINACH AND RICOTTA

**8 TO 10 SERVINGS**

FOR THE CRÊPES:

3 eggs

2 1/2 ounces sifted all-purpose flour

1 1/4 cups milk

salt

melted butter for greasing pan

FOR THE FILLING:

1 pound spinach, boiled, drained, and sautéed in 1/2 ounce unsalted butter

10 ounces fresh ricotta

2 large eggs

2 ounces grated Parmesan cheese

pinch of grated nutmeg

salt and pepper

FOR BAKING:

butter for greasing baking dish

4 tablespoons grated Parmesan cheese

1/2 cup melted butter

To make the crêpes:
Combine the eggs, flour, milk, and a pinch of salt and mix until smooth. Let rest for 15 minutes.

Heat a 9 to 10 inch non-stick crêpe, or similarly shaped pan, over moderately high heat with a little melted butter. Ladle in about 4 tablespoons of batter for each crêpe, swirling it around to evenly coat the pan. Cook until lightly browned on one side. Turn and cook for 5 seconds on the second side. Stack the crêpes as they are cooked and set aside.

To make the filling:
Chop the sautéed spinach and place in a bowl. Add the ricotta, eggs, Parmesan cheese, and grated nutmeg and season with salt and pepper.

Spread the filling over each crêpe and roll each securely.

Place the crêpes, covered with plastic wrap, in the refrigerator for at least 2 hours or overnight.

Preheat the oven to 375° F.

Grease a shallow baking pan. Cut the crêpes into 2-inch rolls. Set the rolls upright, standing in the pan, side by side. Sprinkle with the grated Parmesan cheese and the melted butter.

Cook the crêpes for about 10 minutes. Serve with red sweet pepper fondue (see following recipe).

## FONDUTA AL PEPERONE ROSSO
### RED SWEET PEPPER FONDUE

*8 TO 10 SERVINGS*

2 large red sweet peppers

1 small onion

1/4 cup extra-virgin olive oil

1 cup chicken or beef broth

1 ounce unsalted butter

salt

Place the red peppers in a preheated 375°F oven for 10 to 15 minutes. Remove from the oven and put into a paper bag for 10 minutes. Peel, core, seed, and coarsely chop the peppers.

Thinly slice the onion. Sauté the onion in olive oil in a nonstick frying pan over low heat for 3 minutes. Add the red peppers and broth and cook for about 15 minutes, until almost all of the liquid has evaporated.

Place the red pepper mixture into a blender or food processor and purée. Set aside until ready to serve.

When ready to serve, return the sauce to the pan, stir in the butter, and cook over low heat for 2 to 3 minutes. Season with salt, if needed.

**8 TO 10 SERVINGS**

FOR THE CRÊPES:

3 large eggs

2 1/2 ounces sifted all-purpose flour

1 1/4 cups milk

1 teaspoon salt

melted butter for greasing pan

FOR THE BÉCHAMEL SAUCE:

1/2 cup unsalted butter

1/2 cup all-purpose flour

1 quart heated milk

salt, pepper, and grated nutmeg

7 ounces boiled ham, sliced thick and diced

1/2 pound Emmenthal, diced

FOR THE TOMATO SAUCE:

2 tablespoons extra-virgin olive oil

1 small finely chopped onion

2 garlic cloves, minced

1 pound plum tomatoes, peeled, seeded, and coarsely chopped

5 fresh basil leaves, chopped

salt and pinch pepper

FOR GARNISH:

3/4 pound mozzarella, cut into 1/2-inch cubes

1 teaspoon dried oregano

# CRESPELLE ALLA PIZZAIOLA
## CRÊPES "PIZZAIOLA"

To make the crêpes:

Beat the eggs in a bowl. Add the flour and milk. Beat until smooth. Season with salt. Let rest for 15 minutes. Heat a 9- to 10-inch nonstick pan over moderately high heat. Brush with a little melted butter. Use about 4 tablespoons of batter for each crêpe, swirling it around to evenly coat the pan. Cook until lightly browned on one side, about 1 minute. Turn and cook for 5 seconds on the second side. Stack the crêpes as they are cooked and set aside.

To make the béchamel:

In a small casserole, melt the butter over moderate heat. Remove from heat, add flour and stir until smooth. Return to heat and cook for 1 minute, stirring constantly. Add hot milk, little by little, stirring constantly. Season with salt, pepper, and grated nutmeg. Remove from heat and, when cooled slightly, stir in the diced ham and the Emmenthal. Pour into a bowl and allow to cool at room temperature.

To make the tomato sauce:

Heat the olive oil in a large skillet over moderate heat. Add the onion and garlic and sauté until softened, about 3 minutes. Add the tomato, basil, salt, and a pinch of pepper. Cook until the sauce thickens, about 20 minutes. Set aside.

Preheat the oven to 400° F.

To assemble:

Spread each crêpe evenly with filling. Roll up the crêpes. Trim off the ends and cut each into 3 equal-sized pieces.

Butter the bottom of a large, shallow baking pan. Spread some of the tomato sauce over the bottom and arrange the crêpes, seam side down. Top each one with about 1/2 tablespoon tomato sauce. Put a cube of mozzarella on top of each. Sprinkle with a pinch of oregano.

Bake in the oven until the mozzarella has melted, about 15 minutes. Serve immediately.

# CRESPELLE AL RADICCHIO ROSSO
## CRÊPES WITH RED RADICCHIO

*8 TO 10 SERVINGS*

For the crêpes and béchamel sauce,
see previous recipe (Crêpes "Pizzaiola").

FOR THE FILLING:
1 pound red radicchio
2 tablespoons extra-virgin olive oil
salt and pepper
1/2 tablespoon red wine vinegar
grated Parmesan cheese
unsalted butter

To make the crêpes and béchamel sauce, follow instructions in the previous recipe, without the boiled ham in the béchamel sauce and using a small 5- to 6-inch nonstick pan to make the crêpes.

Wash the radicchio and drain it (some water must remain on leaves).

Place the radicchio, oil, salt, and pepper in a large frying pan and sauté over high heat, stirring constantly, for about 10 minutes. Add the vinegar, lower the heat and cook, covered, for another 5 minutes.

Stir the braised radicchio into the béchamel sauce. Spread the filling over the little crêpes. Fold them in half twice. Place the crêpes in a greased shallow baking pan and dust with grated Parmesan cheese. Dot with little pieces of butter. Cook in a hot oven for 5 to 7 minutes to gratinate.

# RISOTTO AL PROSCIUTTO AFFUMICATO E FINOCCHI
## RISOTTO WITH SMOKED HAM AND FENNEL

Wash the fennel and slice thin, by electric slicing machine, if possible.

Cut the ham slices into strips.

Heat oil in a heavy pan, add chopped onion and cook over low heat until transparent (if needed, add a little hot broth to prevent onion from browning).

Add the fennel and ham and cook 7 to 8 minutes, adding some more hot broth. Reserve 2 tablespoons of this mixture.

Add the rice to the pan. Stir well and sauté on high heat for 1 minute.

Add the wine and season with salt and pepper. Let the wine evaporate and continue cooking, adding the boiling vegetable broth, 1/2 cup at a time, stirring constantly, for about 15 minutes.

Add the 2 tablespoons of the reserved fennel and ham mixture and cook for another 5 minutes.

Remove from heat, and vigorously stir in the Parmesan cheese and butter.

Cover the pan and let rest for a couple of minutes before serving.

### 6 SERVINGS

1 large fennel bulb

3 1/2 ounces smoked ham,
cut into 1/4-inch-thick slices

1/4 cup extra-virgin olive oil

1 small white onion, finely chopped

1 pound Arborio or other short-grain rice

1/2 cup dry white wine

salt and pepper

1 quart vegetable broth

2 ounces grated Parmesan cheese

1 ounce unsalted butter

## RISOTTO CON LE MELE (O LE PERE)
RISOTTO WITH APPLES (OR PEARS)

Melt the butter in a casserole with the chopped onion and let cook gently over low heat until the onion is soft and transparent.

Add the rice, and let it brown, stirring well, for 3 minutes. Add the white wine and continue to stir the rice until the wine has evaporated. Add a cup of hot broth and the apples (or the pears). Stir and continue adding the broth, 1/2 cup at a time, until the liquid has been absorbed and the risotto is done (about 15 minutes). Season with salt and pepper.

A few minutes before the end of cooking, add the Gorgonzola cheese in small pieces, and the parsley, and stir well.

Serve hot and sprinkle with grated Parmesan cheese if desired.

*6 SERVINGS*

2 ounces unsalted butter

1 small white onion, finely chopped

1 pound Arborio or other short-grain rice

1/2 cup dry white wine

1 quart vegetable broth

1 pound apples (or pears),
peeled, cored, and diced

salt and pepper

7 ounces Gorgonzola

2 tablespoons fresh chopped parsley

grated Parmesan cheese

## ZUPPA DI CIPOLLE BIANCHE NEL COCCIO
### WHITE ONION SOUP IN CROCKS

Peel the onions and cut into very thin slices.

Put the onions into a casserole, add the oil and a pinch of salt. Cover and cook over very low heat for about 1/2 hour. Remove from heat.

In a 350°F oven, lightly toast the flour on a baking tray for 5 minutes. Add the flour to the braised onions. Pour in the broth, stirring well.

Return to the heat again and bring the soup to a boil. Cook over moderate heat for another 1/2 hour.

Melt the butter in an iron skillet and quickly sauté the bread slices.

When the soup is ready, ladle into 6 individual crocks. Top each crock of soup with 2 slices of sautéed bread. Finish with a slice of fontina and sprinkle with Parmesan cheese.

Put the crocks of soup on a baking tray and pass under the broiler for a minute or two to melt the cheese and lightly brown the tops.

*6 SERVINGS*

3 large white onions
1 tablespoon extra-virgin olive oil
salt
1 tablespoon all-purpose flour
1 quart beef broth
1 ounce unsalted butter
12 thin slices Tuscan or country bread
6 thin slices fontina
grated Parmesan cheese

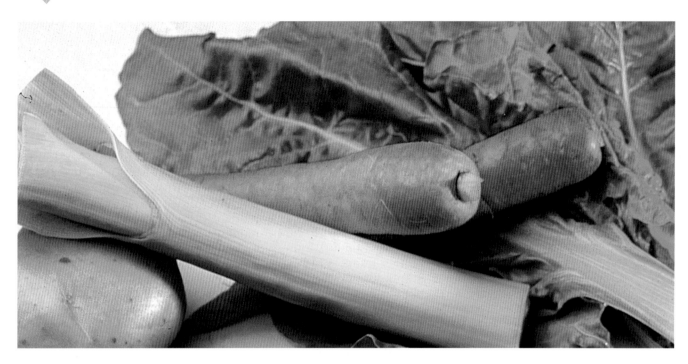

## MINESTRA D'ORZO
### BARLEY SOUP

*8 SERVINGS*

4 ounces speck or smoked ham,
cut into 1/4-inch-thick slices

2 carrots, peeled

1 leek (white part only)

5 ounces unsalted butter

2 medium-sized boiling potatoes

4 ounces fresh Swiss chard

1/2 pound pearl barley

2 quarts heated beef stock

1 celery stalk

grated Parmesan cheese

Dice the speck or ham slices and the carrot. Slice the leek very thin.

Melt the butter in a pot over medium heat, add the speck, carrot, and leek and cook for 2 minutes.

Meantime, peel the potatoes and cut into 3/4-inch cubes. Wash the Swiss chard and coarsely chop it.

Put the above ingredients into the pot, add the barley, and let cook for another 3 minutes, stirring continuously.

Add the hot beef stock and the celery stalk. Bring to a boil over high heat. Cover and reduce the heat to very low. Let it simmer for 1 1/2 hours. Discard the celery stalk.

Before serving, if necessary, season with salt.

Pass the Parmesan cheese.

## ZUPPA DI FUNGHI E PATATE
### MUSHROOM AND POTATO SOUP

Peel and cut the potatoes into 1/2-inch cubes.

Heat the butter in a large saucepan and add the onion and let cook over low heat, covered, for about 10 minutes, adding some hot water to prevent burning. The onion must become transparent.

Add the smoked ham and the potatoes. Mix well and cook about 2 minutes.

Pour in the hot broth and hot milk and a pinch of grated nutmeg. Season with salt and pepper.

Stir the mushrooms into the soup and bring it to a boil. Immediately lower the heat, cover, and simmer for 20 minutes.

Put half of the soup into a blender (in two batches) and process. Pour the puréed soup back into the saucepan, stir well, and bring back to a boil. Remove from heat.

Toast the bread and rub lightly with garlic.

Place 1 slice of toasted bread on the bottom of each of 8 soup plates. Ladle the soup over the bread and serve immediately.

Pass the Parmesan cheese.

*8 SERVINGS*

1 1/2 pounds boiling potatoes

1 1/2 ounces unsalted butter

1 medium-sized white onion, finely sliced

5 ounces smoked ham, diced

1 quart heated beef stock

1 1/2 cups heated milk

grated nutmeg

salt and pepper

1/2 pound fresh porcini mushrooms, thinly sliced

8 slices Italian country bread

1 garlic clove, halved

grated Parmesan cheese

*8 TO 10 SERVINGS*

1 pound dried cannellini or navy beans

5 tablespoons extra-virgin olive oil

2 cloves garlic, chopped

3 boiling potatoes,
peeled and coarsely chopped

2 sprigs of fresh sage

3 large plum tomatoes,
peeled, seeded, and chopped

10 ounces short cut pasta (ditali)

salt and pepper

# PASTA E FAGIOLI
## PASTA AND BEAN SOUP

Cover the beans with cold water and soak for 12 hours. Drain.

Heat 3 tablespoons of olive oil in a pot over moderate heat. Add half of the garlic, potatoes, and half the sage. Sauté for 5 minutes, stirring frequently. Add the tomatoes and cook for 5 more minutes.

Add the beans and enough boiling water to cover by about 1 inch. Simmer over moderate heat until the beans are tender, about 1 1/2 hours.

Remove 3 cups of beans and potatoes with a slotted spoon. Purée in a blender or food processor. Set aside.

In a small frying pan, sauté the remaining garlic and sage in 2 tablespoons of olive oil over medium heat for 3 minutes. Stir into the puréed beans. Set aside.

Bring the soup back to a boil, stir in the pasta and cook until al dente, about 15 minutes. Stir in the bean purée. Season with salt and pepper. Add a little water if the soup is too thick. Serve immediately.

## MINESTRA DI RISO E SPINACI
### RICE AND SPINACH SOUP

*8 SERVINGS*

4 fresh sage leaves

1 celery stalk

2 tablespoons chopped parsley

2 tablespoons extra-virgin olive oil

1 ounce unsalted butter

1 clove garlic

10 ounces fresh spinach

6 cups heated beef broth

6 ounces Arborio or other short-grain rice

1 cup heated milk

salt and pepper

1 egg, plus 2 egg yolks

2 tablespoons grated Parmesan cheese

Finely chop the sage, celery, and add half of the parsley.

Heat oil and butter in a saucepan with the clove of garlic, chopped sage, celery, and parsley. Cook gently for 2 to 3 minutes.

Add the spinach, washed, drained, and coarsely chopped. Cook, stirring often, 5 to 6 minutes over medium heat, without burning.

Pour in the hot broth and continue cooking for 10 minutes over medium heat.

Add the rice and cook over medium-high heat until rice is tender, about 15 minutes.

Pour in the cup of milk. Season with salt and pepper.

Beat the egg and egg yolks together with the Parmesan cheese in a bowl with the remaining parsley.

Remove soup from heat. Pour the egg mixture into the soup, quickly stirring to blend well.

Serve immediately.

# SUGGESTED WINES

FOR BEEF AND GAME:

**Lodola Nuova** - Nobile di Montepulciano **Ruffino**

Barolo

Merlot delle Grave del Friuli

Brunello di Montalcino

**Cabreo Il Borgo** - Sangiovese - Cabernet **Ruffino**


FOR VEAL AND PORK:

**Santedame** - Chianti Classico **Ruffino**

Barbera

Aglianico del Vulture

**Riserva Ducale** - Chianti Classico **Ruffino**

# $\mathcal{M}$EAT

## PICCATINA DI VITELLA AL CARTOCCIO
### VEAL SCALLOPS BAKED IN FOIL

To make the sauce:
Heat the olive oil, garlic, and basil in a skillet over moderate heat for about 3 minutes. Add the tomatoes, salt, and a pinch of pepper. Simmer about 20 minutes, stirring occasionally.

Flatten each piece of veal very thin.

Preheat the oven to 450° F.

Melt the butter in a large frying pan.

Lightly dust the veal scallops with flour and sauté very quickly on both sides over high heat. Season with salt and pepper.

Remove the scallops and drain on paper towels.

Cut the mozzarella into 6 slices.

Grease the foil with butter and place 2 slices of veal on each square of foil. Cover the veal with a little tomato sauce, a slice of mozzarella, and 4 crushed capers.

Close the foil squares securely by folding sides and cook in the oven on a baking sheet for 5 to 7 minutes. Transfer the sealed cartocci to a platter and serve immediately.

*6 SERVINGS*

FOR THE TOMATO SAUCE:
2 tablespoons extra-virgin olive oil
1 clove garlic
15 fresh basil leaves
1 pound ripe tomatoes,
peeled, seeded, and coarsely chopped
salt and pepper
12 thin veal scallops (6 ounces each)
2 ounces unsalted butter,
plus extra for greasing foil
all-purpose flour for dusting
salt and pepper
1/2 pound mozzarella
24 capers
6 squares of foil, each 10 by 10 inches

## 6 SERVINGS

1 pound red radicchio, leaves separated

3 tablespoons extra-virgin olive oil

salt and pepper

1/2 tablespoon red wine vinegar

4 ounces unsalted butter

18 thin slices veal rump

9 thin slices prosciutto

9 thin slices fontina

1/2 small white onion, finely diced

all-purpose flour for dusting

1/2 cup red wine

# INVOLTINI DI VITELLA AL RADICCHIO ROSSO
## VEAL ROLLS STUFFED WITH RED RADICCHIO

Wash the radicchio and quickly drain (some water must remain on leaves). Cut the biggest leaves in half.

Put the radicchio in a large skillet with 2 tablespoons of the oil, and season with salt and pepper. Sauté over high heat, always stirring, for about 10 minutes.

Add the vinegar, and 1 ounce of the butter. Lower the heat and cook, covered, for another 5 minutes. Let cool.

Gently flatten the veal slices. There must be no breaks or holes in the meat.

In the center of each piece of veal, place half a slice of prosciutto, then half a slice of fontina, and top with a small amount of the cooked radicchio.

Tightly roll up the veal from one end to the other, lengthwise, and secure with a toothpick.

Put the onion and remaining butter into a large saucepan. Add the remaining oil and cook over medium heat until the onion is tender, but not brown (3 to 4 minutes).

Quickly dust the veal rolls with a little flour. Place them into the saucepan with the onion mixture. Brown them well, carefully turning, one by one.

Add the red wine and cook, covered, for about 15 minutes, stirring occasionally, over low heat.

When done, transfer the veal rolls to a warmed serving dish. Remove the toothpicks. Spoon the sauce over the rolls and serve hot.

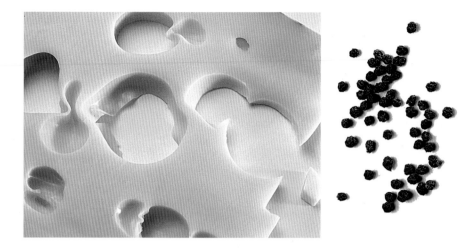

## SCALOPPINE AL MARSALA GRATINATE
### AU GRATIN OF VEAL SCALLOPS WITH MARSALA

*6 SERVINGS*

1 1/2 pounds veal scallops, thinly sliced

2 tablespoons extra-virgin olive oil

2 ounces unsalted butter

salt and pepper

1 tablespoon all-purpose flour

1/2 cup vegetable broth

2 tablespoons Marsala wine

2 ounces sliced boiled ham, cut into thin strips

2 tablespoons grated Parmesan cheese

2 tablespoons grated Emmenthal cheese

Flatten veal scallops as thin as possible without breaking the skin.

Heat the oil and butter in a large frying pan. Sauté the scallops on each side, season with salt and pepper, and arrange in a greased, shallow baking pan.

In the frying pan where the scallops were cooked, stir in the flour, broth, and Marsala wine, and let reduce over high heat, stirring constantly.

Pour the sauce over the veal scallops.

Sprinkle the top with the ham and the Parmesan and Emmenthal cheeses.

A few minutes before serving, pass under a hot broiler for a few minutes to brown the top slightly.

**6 SERVINGS**

6 veal cutlets (about 9 ounces each)

1 small white truffle, thinly sliced

2 ounces Parmesan cheese, shaved

salt

all-purpose flour

2 ounces unsalted butter,
plus extra for greasing pan

pepper

1 tablespoon dry white wine

1/4 cup beef broth

1 small black truffle, cut into 6 slices

# COTOLETTA DI VITELLA TARTUFATA
## VEAL CUTLETS WITH TRUFFLES

Flatten veal cutlets very thin.

Put equal amounts of the white truffle slices and a few shavings of half of the Parmesan cheese in the center of each cutlet.

Fold one side of each veal cutlet over the truffle and Parmesan cheese to the opposite edge of meat. Gently pound the edges together to seal. Season each cutlet with salt and dust lightly with flour.

Heat the butter in a large skillet and sauté the cutlets for about 4 minutes on each side. Season with pepper.

Remove excess fat from the pan. Add the wine and the beef broth. Let simmer 4 more minutes.

Transfer the cutlets to a greased, shallow baking dish. Put 1 slice of black truffle and a few remaining Parmesan cheese shavings on top of each cutlet. Spoon the sauce over the cutlets. Cook in a preheated 400°F oven for about 3 minutes. Serve very hot.

## ARROSTO ARROTOLATO
### ROLLED VEAL OR TURKEY BREAST

Flatten the piece of meat with a mallet and season it with salt and pepper.

Heat 1 ounce of the butter with 1 tablespoon of the oil in a 7-inch nonstick omelet or other round pan.

Beat the eggs and pour into the pan. Cook until browned lightly on one side. Remove from the heat.

Cover the flattened meat with the boiled ham and the omelet.

Roll up the meat nice and tight and tie with kitchen string. Fit the sage leaves under the string at equal distances apart.

Put 4 tablespoons of oil and 1 ounce of the butter into a large, deep saucepan. Over medium-high heat, brown the roast on all sides, about 10 minutes. Add the broth, reduce the heat, and cook, covered, for about 30 minutes.

Add the wine, cover, and simmer for 5 minutes.

Transfer the roast to a warmed platter.

Work the softened butter and cornstarch together with your fingers or a fork.

Add the mixture to the sauce in the pot and cook at a low boil for about 2 minutes, stirring often.

Remove string from the meat. Carve the meat into thin slices and arrange on a serving dish. Spoon the hot sauce over the top.

*8 TO 10 SERVINGS*

1 1/2 pounds boneless veal
or turkey breast, in one piece
(about 7 to 10 inches long and 1 inch thick)

salt and pepper

2 ounces unsalted butter,
plus 1 teaspoon softened butter

1/3 cup extra-virgin olive oil

2 large eggs

3 ounces boiled ham, thinly sliced

4 fresh sage leaves

1 cup chicken broth

1/2 cup dry white wine

1 teaspoon cornstarch

# INVOLTINI RIPIENI DI CARCIOFI
## ROLLED VEAL SCALLOPS STUFFED WITH ARTICHOKES

Flatten the veal scallops and set aside.

Remove the artichokes' tough outer leaves and center. Cut each heart into quarters. Soak them for 5 minutes in cold water with the lemon juice. Pat the artichoke pieces dry.

Mince the prosciutto and mix with 1 tablespoon of butter to make a smooth, spreadable mixture. Lightly season with salt and pepper.

Spread the mixture over each artichoke piece and place in the center of each slice of meat; roll up tightly and secure with a toothpick.

Put the onion, remaining butter, and oil in a saucepan and cook over medium heat until onion is translucent.

Dust the veal rolls lightly with flour and arrange in the saucepan.

Brown over high heat for a few minutes. Pour in the wine. Lower the heat. Add 1/2 cup of the broth, cover, and simmer for about 30 minutes.

When done, remove the veal rolls from the saucepan. Discard the toothpicks and arrange on a warm serving dish.

Mix the remaining 1/2 cup of the broth with the sauce in the pan and bring to a boil. Cook a minute or two, then pour the sauce over the veal.

*4 SERVINGS*

8 thin veal scallops (6 ounces each)

2 large fresh artichokes

juice of half a lemon

2 ounces prosciutto, thinly sliced

2 tablespoons unsalted butter

salt and pepper

1 small onion, finely chopped

1 tablespoon extra-virgin olive oil

all-purpose flour

1/2 cup dry white wine

1 cup chicken broth

## PETTO DI TACCHINO AGLI AROMI
### TURKEY BREAST STUFFED WITH VEAL AND AROMATIC HERBS

Preheat the oven to 375°F.

Soak the bread in the milk and squeeze to dampness.

Cut the veal into small pieces and put into the food processor with the dampened bread, parsley, and chervil. Process for about 1 minute.

Transfer to a bowl and add the eggs, salt and pepper to taste, a pinch of nutmeg, and Parmesan cheese.

Line the turkey with slices of boiled ham and top with the veal mixture.

Roll the meat up tightly and tie it with kitchen string.

Lightly grease a sheet of foil with olive oil. Wrap the stuffed turkey breast in the foil. Cook on a baking sheet in the oven for 20 minutes. Turn the roll, and cook for another 20 minutes.

Remove the turkey from the oven. Discard the foil and string. Carve into thin slices.

*6 SERVINGS*

2 ounces soft part of bread

1/2 cup warm milk

1/2 pound lean veal

1 tablespoon each freshly chopped parsley and chervil

2 large eggs

salt and pepper

freshly grated nutmeg

3 tablespoons grated Parmesan cheese

One 2-pound boneless turkey breast, cut into a large 6 by 8-inch piece, flattened to 1 inch thick

4 thin slices boiled ham

olive oil for greasing foil

# FILETTO AL PEPE VERDE
## FILLET OF BEEF WITH GREEN PEPPERCORN SAUCE

Place the meat with the peppercorns, oil, onion, pieces of butter, and vinegar in a casserole. Let it marinate about 1 hour, turning occasionally.

Turn the heat on high and cook for about 10 minutes, browning the ingredients, turning the meat on all sides.

Pour in half of the wine, season with salt and pepper, lower the heat, and cook for 10 minutes over medium heat. Add the remaining wine and cook about 5 minutes, turning meat occasionally.

Remove the fillet from the pan and let cool for 15 minutes.

Discard the string and carve the meat into thin slices. Arrange slices on a warmed serving platter and spoon the heated green peppercorn sauce over the top.

*8 TO 10 SERVINGS*

2 pounds beef fillet, tied up

2 tablespoons green peppercorns

1/4 cup extra-virgin olive oil

1 small onion, thinly chopped

1 ounce unsalted butter, cut into small pieces

2 tablespoons red wine vinegar

3/4 cup dry white wine (Orvieto)

salt and pepper

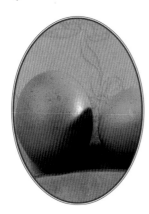

## CONIGLIO IN SALSA D'UOVO
### RABBIT WITH EGG YOLK AND LEMON SAUCE

Wash the rabbit well under cool running water. Pat it dry. Cut into 1-inch pieces, including the bones.

Heat the butter and oil in a casserole. When hot, add the rabbit and cook over high heat for 4 minutes, stirring often. Add the chopped onion, mix well, and season with salt and pepper. Add the prosciutto and 1 tablespoon of the chopped parsley. Stir well and let brown. Stir in wine. Sprinkle the flour over the ingredients; add enough hot water to barely cover the rabbit.

Cover and lower heat to a simmer. Cook for about 1 hour, or until the meat is tender when pierced with a fork, stirring occasionally.

To prepare the sauce, beat the egg yolks in a bowl. Beat in the lemon juice and remaining parsley.

Just before serving, reheat the rabbit briefly. Take the casserole off the heat and, little by little, stir in the sauce. Cover. Let rest for 5 minutes before serving.

*6 TO 8 SERVINGS*

One 3 1/2-pound rabbit
1 tablespoon unsalted butter
3 tablespoons extra-virgin olive oil
1 tablespoon finely chopped onion
salt and pepper
8 thin slices prosciutto, chopped
2 tablespoons chopped parsley
1/2 cup dry white wine
1/2 tablespoon all-purpose flour
3 egg yolks
juice of 1 lemon

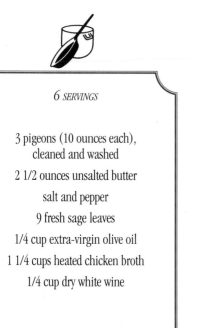

## PICCIONI STUFATI
### STEWED PIGEONS

Dry pigeons well.

Work butter together with salt and pepper to taste. Place equal amounts inside pigeons with 3 sage leaves each. Truss the pigeons.

Pour the oil into a casserole and add the pigeons. Let cook over high heat, turning to brown lightly on all sides. Add the hot broth, 1/4 cup at a time, and cook covered over moderate heat for about 1 1/2 hours.

Add the wine and cook for about 5 minutes.

Transfer the pigeons to a cutting board. Discard the trussing string. Cut each pigeon in half. Arrange the pigeons on a warm serving dish and spoon the sauce over the top.

*6 SERVINGS*

3 pigeons (10 ounces each), cleaned and washed

2 1/2 ounces unsalted butter

salt and pepper

9 fresh sage leaves

1/4 cup extra-virgin olive oil

1 1/4 cups heated chicken broth

1/4 cup dry white wine

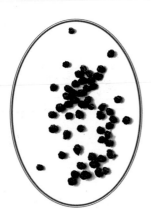

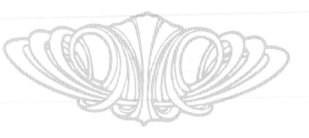

## CROCCHETTE DI POLLO AI FUNGHI
### CHICKEN CROQUETTES WITH MUSHROOMS

*6 SERVINGS*

1 ounce dried porcini mushrooms

2 tablespoons extra-virgin olive oil

2 ounces unsalted butter

1 garlic clove, minced

2 ounces prosciutto, thinly sliced

1 1/2 pounds boneless and skinless boiled or roasted chicken

2 large eggs

2 tablespoons grated Parmesan cheese

1/2 cup freshly chopped parsley

grated zest of 1 lemon

salt and pepper

pinch of freshly grated nutmeg

all-purpose flour

1/2 cup chicken broth

juice of half a lemon

Soak the mushrooms in lukewarm water for 15 minutes. Drain and squeeze out water. Mince the mushrooms.

Heat 1 tablespoon each of the oil and butter in a frying pan and add the garlic and mushrooms. Cook over medium heat for 3 to 4 minutes, stirring often. Remove from the heat and let cool.

Mince the prosciutto and chicken. Place in a bowl with the eggs, mushroom mixture, Parmesan cheese, parsley, and lemon zest. Mix well and season with salt, pepper, and nutmeg.

Shape the mixture into 12 small, equal-sized balls, then flatten them slightly. Dust with flour.

Heat the remaining butter and oil in a large skillet and fry the croquettes on both sides until golden. Add 1/3 cup of the broth, cover and simmer for 10 to 15 minutes.

Transfer the croquettes to a warm serving platter.

Over medium-high heat, add the lemon juice and remaining chicken broth to the pan. Reduce slightly, then pour over the croquettes and serve immediately.

## VITELLO ALLA BRESCIANA
### VEAL BRAISED IN EXTRA-VIRGIN OLIVE OIL

*8 TO 10 SERVINGS*

3 pounds veal rump

3/4 cup extra-virgin olive oil

2 tablespoons red wine vinegar

4 anchovy fillets, chopped

1 small onion, chopped

1 carrot, peeled and chopped

2 cloves garlic

1 celery stalk, chopped

2 cups beef broth

2 tablespoons dried bread crumbs

3 tablespoons grated Parmesan cheese

Tie the veal rump up with kitchen string and place in a casserole with the ingredients from the olive oil through the celery stalk. Let the veal rest in the marinade for at least 1 hour, turning occasionally.

Add the beef stock, cover the casserole with a tight-fitting lid, and cook over very low heat for 2 hours. Turn meat occasionally during cooking time, always covering the casserole again.

Remove the meat from the casserole to a warm dish and cover with foil.

Put the ingredients and liquid from the pan into a blender or food processor with the bread crumbs and Parmesan cheese. Process for 1 minute.

Transfer the veal to a carving board. Discard the string and carve the veal into thin slices. Arrange the slices on an ovenproof serving dish. Spoon the sauce over the slices and heat in a 375° F preheated oven for 3 to 4 minutes before serving.

## MANZO STUFATO
### STEWED BEEF

Tie beef with kitchen string and dust evenly with flour.

Put the olive oil, butter, and onion in a casserole and cook until onion is transparent.

Add the beef and brown on all sides. Season with salt and pepper.

Add the vinegar and let evaporate a minute or two. Add the tomato sauce and enough wine to just cover the beef. Add the cloves.

Cook, covered, over low heat, for 2 1/2 hours, turning occasionally, adding a little water, if necessary.

Near the end of cooking time, stir in the sugar.

Remove from the heat and let rest for 10 to 15 minutes.

Discard string and carve the beef into 1/2-inch-thick slices. Arrange on a warm serving dish and spoon the heated sauce over the top.

*8 TO 10 SERVINGS*

3 pounds beef rump

all-purpose flour for dusting

3 tablespoons extra-virgin olive oil

1 ounce butter

1 medium-sized onion, chopped

salt and pepper

3 tablespoons red wine vinegar

2 tablespoons tomato sauce

1 bottle Chianti Classico

3 or 4 cloves

1 teaspoon sugar

## LEPRE SFILATA
### STEWED HARE

Cut the hare into serving pieces. Wash with water mixed with a little vinegar. Pat dry with paper towels.

Crush the peppercorns and juniper berries. Put them into a large bowl with the vegetables, bay leaf, and herbs and mix well.

Place half of the marinade mixture into another large bowl. Top with the hare pieces and cover with the remaining marinade mixture. Pour in the wine. Cover the bowl with plastic wrap and refrigerate for 24 hours.

When ready to cook, heat the olive oil with the butter in a deep frying pan and sauté the onion and pancetta a few minutes.

Dust the hare pieces lightly with flour and sauté until well browned on each side.

Season with salt and pepper and pour in the marinade and wine. Cover the pan and braise over low heat for about 2 hours, stirring occasionally.

When the meat starts to fall off the bones, remove pan from the heat. Remove the hare pieces.

Pass the cooking sauce through a food mill. Return it to the pot and simmer for a few minutes. Taste for seasoning.

Meanwhile, remove the meat from the bones, shredding it with your fingers with the grain of the meat.

Return the meat to the pot. Simmer for a few minutes and serve very hot with polenta.

*6 TO 8 SERVINGS*

One 4-pound hare
vinegar

FOR THE MARINADE:

8 whole black peppercorns

5 juniper berries

1 large onion, chopped

3 carrots, peeled and chopped

1 celery stalk, chopped

2 cloves garlic, chopped

1 bay leaf

pinch each of thyme and marjoram

1 bottle red wine (Chianti)

3 tablespoons extra-virgin olive oil

2 ounces unsalted butter

1 medium-sized onion, thinly sliced

4 ounces smoked pancetta or bacon, diced

all-purpose flour for dusting

salt and pepper

## ARISTA DI MAIALE ALLA SENAPE
PORK ROAST IN MUSTARD SAUCE

*8 TO 10 SERVINGS*

One 3-pound lean, boneless pork roast
1 fresh rosemary sprig
1 small white onion, finely chopped
4 ounces unsalted butter
1/4 cup Dijon mustard
salt and pepper
2 cups hot milk

Tie up the pork roast and insert the rosemary sprig under the string.

Lightly brown the onion in the butter in a casserole.

Rub the pork with 3 tablespoons of the mustard and put into the casserole. Brown the roast on all sides. Sprinkle with salt and pepper and add the hot milk. Cook, covered, over low heat for about 1 hour, turning occasionally during cooking time.

Remove the pork from the casserole. Discard string and rosemary. Carve pork into thin slices and arrange on warm serving dish.

Stir the remaining mustard into the sauce in the pan and cook for a minute or two. Spoon the sauce over the pork.

## ARISTA CON LE PRUGNE
### FLORENTINE ROAST PORK WITH PRUNES

Preheat the oven to 350° F.

Bone the pork. Chop the bones coarsely.

Peel the garlic cloves and cut each in half. Make little incisions in six places in the meat and insert half a garlic clove in each. Season the pork well with salt and pepper and tie up with kitchen string.

Put the roast into an ovenproof baking pan with the olive oil. Arrange the chopped bones around it. Over high heat, brown the meat well on all sides and stir the bones. Place in the oven and cook for about 1 1/2 hours.

Meanwhile, soak the prunes, covered with cold water, for 20 minutes. Drain and remove the pit from each. Add the prunes to the roasting pan for the last 30 minutes of cooking time.

Halve the apples. As you core them, be sure to make a hole big enough to hold a prune comfortably.

Boil the apple halves, covered with water mixed with the lemon juice, for about 10 minutes or just until tender.

Drain the apples and reserve.

When the pork is done, remove it from the baking pan. Discard the string. Cover it with foil and set aside.

Remove 8 prunes from the pan and place in the center of each apple half.

Over low heat, cook the juice in the pan until it begins to stick slightly. Drain off the fat.

Stir the wine into the pan and let it evaporate for a minute or two. Add 1/4 cup of water and simmer for about 10 minutes.

Discard the bones. Purée the remaining sauce and prunes in a blender.

Carve the pork into thin slices and arrange on a warm serving platter. Garnish with the prune-stuffed apples. Spoon the hot sauce over the pork.

*8 SERVINGS*

One 3-pound lean pork loin, with the bones

3 cloves garlic

salt and pepper

1/4 cup extra-virgin olive oil

10 ounces prunes

4 small baking apples

juice of 1 lemon

1/2 cup dry white wine

## POLLO ALLA SUPRÊME
### CHICKEN SUPRÊME

Truss the chicken.

Put the chicken, vegetables, parsley, and peppercorns into a large pot and season with salt. Cover with cool water. Bring to a boil. Immediately reduce the heat and simmer for about 1 hour or until chicken is tender.

Transfer the chicken to a dish and cover with foil to keep warm.

To make the suprême sauce:
Melt the butter in a saucepan. Whisk in the flour and cook for about 2 minutes over low heat, stirring often. Season with salt.

Over low heat, and constantly stirring, slowly pour in the hot chicken broth and cook about 10 minutes.

Remove the sauce from the heat. Combine the egg yolks with the lemon juice, and slowly add to the sauce, constantly stirring. Add the Parmesan cheese and blend into the sauce. Cover the surface of the sauce with plastic wrap and keep warm in the top pan of a double boiler over hot water in the lower pan.

Skin and bone the chicken. Separate the meat into pieces and cover to keep warm.

Pass all the remaining broth and ingredients in the pot through a sieve or food mill. Return it to the pot and bring to a boil. Add the rice and cook for 20 minutes or until done.

Drain the rice well. Spoon it into a warm serving dish. Arrange the chicken pieces on top of the rice. Spoon a generous amount of the suprême sauce over the chicken and rice. Serve immediately. Pass the extra sauce in a bowl.

*6 TO 8 SERVINGS*

One 4-to 5-pound chicken

2 carrots, peeled

1 medium-size onion peeled

1 celery stalk

4 sprigs fresh parsley

6 peppercorns

salt

1 pound Arborio or other short-grain rice

FOR THE SUPRÊME SAUCE:

4 ounces unsalted butter

4 ounces all-purpose flour

salt

1 quart hot chicken broth

3 egg yolks

juice of 3 lemons

3 tablespoons grated Parmesan cheese

# BRASATO DI VITELLA AL LATTE
## VEAL BRAISED IN MILK

*8 TO 10 SERVINGS*

One 2 1/2-pound boneless veal roast
1 tablespoon mustard
pepper
1 teaspoon salt, plus a pinch
1/4 teaspoon powdered saffron
2 ounces unsalted butter
1 clove garlic, peeled
2 cups milk
1 beef bouillon cube
1/2 cup sour cream

Tie the veal with a string.

Combine the mustard, pepper, 1 teaspoon salt, and half of the saffron. Brush this mixture over the veal.

Melt the butter in a casserole over high heat. Add the garlic and meat. Reduce the heat to low and brown the veal on all sides for about 20 minutes.

Heat the milk in a saucepan. Slowly add it to the casserole with the veal. Cook for about 1 hour, covered, turning the meat occasionally.

When the veal is done, remove it from the pan. Cover with foil to keep warm.

Pour the sauce from the casserole into a saucepan and heat over low heat. Add the bouillon cube and the rest of the saffron and bring to a boil. Cook until the sauce is reduced to half. Stir in the sour cream and season with salt.

Remove the string from the veal and carve into thin slices. Spoon the hot sauce over the veal and serve immediately.

## POLPETTONE AL BASILICO
### VEAL AND CHICKEN MEAT LOAF WITH BASIL

Preheat the oven to 375° F.

Soak the soft white bread in the milk for 2 minutes. Squeeze out the milk and put into a large bowl with the meat, eggs, Parmesan cheese, and 2 tablespoons of the dried bread crumbs.

Cut the basil leaves into very thin strips and add to the mixture. Season with salt, pepper, and nutmeg.

Work mixture together with the hands and form into a large sausage shape. Coat it with the remaining bread crumbs.

Grease a square of foil with olive oil. Wrap the meat loaf in the foil.

Put it onto a baking sheet and cook in the oven for 40 minutes, turning once halfway through cooking time.

Remove the meat loaf from the oven and carefully remove the foil.

Cut into slices and serve hot.

NOTE: If you want to serve this dish cold, accompany it with mayonnaise or tomato vinaigrette. To make the tomato vinaigrette: Purée 2 to 3 peeled and seeded ripe tomatoes with the juice of half a lemon and 3 tablespoons of extra-virgin olive oil in a food processor. Season with salt and pepper.

*6 TO 8 SERVINGS*

2 ounces soft part of white bread
1/4 cup milk
1/2 pound ground veal
1/2 pound ground chicken breast
1/4 pound ground boiled ham
2 eggs
2 ounces grated Parmesan cheese
1/4 cup dried bread crumbs
20 fresh basil leaves
salt and pepper
grated nutmeg
extra-virgin olive oil for greasing foil

## VITELLO TONNATO
### VEAL WITH TUNA SAUCE

Preheat the oven to 375° F.

To make the roast:
Tie the roast with kitchen string and dust lightly with flour.

Brown the roast in a rather small ovenproof pan, with the oil and garlic. When the meat is browned on all sides, remove the garlic, season with salt and pepper, and add the wine. Let the wine evaporate a few minutes. Place dabs of butter on the meat and cook in the oven about 50 minutes. Check to see if liquid has evaporated; add some broth if necessary. When the meat is cooked, remove it from the oven and let it cool. This part of the preparation can be done 1 day before you serve the vitello tonnato. Cover and refrigerate overnight.

To make the sauce:
Place the drained tuna, anchovy paste, broth, and the capers in a food processor. Process until you obtain a creamy sauce.

Put the mayonnaise into a bowl. Add the processed tuna mixture, a little at a time, mixing it well with a rubber spatula.

Cut the cold meat into thin slices and place on a large serving platter. Spread the tuna sauce over the meat and garnish with capers.

*8 SERVINGS*

One 1 1/2-pound veal roast

all-purpose flour

3 tablespoons extra-virgin olive oil

1 clove garlic, peeled

salt and pepper

1/2 cup dry white wine

2 ounces unsalted butter, softened

1 cup vegetable broth, or as needed

TUNA SAUCE:

7 ounces olive-oil-packed canned tuna

1 tablespoon anchovy paste

2 tablespoons vegetable broth

3 tablespoons capers,
plus extra tablespoon for garnish

1/2 cup mayonnaise

# VEGETABLE SIDE DISHES

*8 SERVINGS*

2 pounds baking potatoes

butter for greasing dish

2 large eggs

1 cup milk

3/4 cup heavy cream

3 1/2 ounces sliced boiled ham,
cut into thin strips

2 ounces grated Parmesan cheese

nutmeg

salt and pepper

## PATATE AL FORNO
### BAKED POTATO PIE

Preheat the oven to 350° F.

Peel the potatoes and cut them evenly into 1/2-inch-thick slices.

Grease a 9- to 10-inch round baking dish with butter. Arrange the potato slices neatly in the dish, slightly overlapping each other in rows.

Beat the eggs, milk, cream, ham, Parmesan cheese, and grated nutmeg together well. Add salt and pepper to taste.

Pour the mixture over the potatoes and bake in the oven for 30 to 40 minutes, until golden brown on top.

# PATATE FARCITE AL FORMAGGIO
## BAKED POTATOES STUFFED WITH CHEESE

Wash the potatoes. Peel and cut them in half lengthwise. Scoop out a hole in the center of each, leaving about 1/3 inch raw potato, to make shells.

Preheat the oven to 375°F.

Grease a shallow baking dish well and arrange the potatoes in it, cut sides up. Lightly salt and brush the inside of each potato with melted butter.

Bake in the oven for 45 minutes.

Meantime, prepare the filling:
Combine the two egg yolks, the creamy cheese, 2/3 of the grated cheeses, aromatic herbs, and the parsley. Season with salt and pepper. Beat the egg white and fold gently into the cheese mixture.

Remove potatoes from oven. Put a rounded tablespoon of cheese mixture into the center of each potato. Sprinkle the top with the remaining combined grated cheeses and a little melted butter.

Place under the broiler for 2 to 3 minutes or until the top is golden brown.

### 8 SERVINGS

2 pounds medium-sized baking potatoes

1 ounce melted unsalted butter, plus extra for greasing dish

salt and pepper

1 large egg (separated) plus 1 egg yolk

2 ounces Certosa cheese
(or other soft, mild cheese, such as cream cheese)

2 ounces grated Parmesan cheese

2 ounces grated Gruyère cheese

1 teaspoon dried thyme

1 teaspoon dried marjoram

2 teaspoons chopped fresh parsley

## PATATE ALLA CASALINGA
### POTATOES HOUSEWIFE STYLE

*8 SERVINGS*

6 tablespoons extra-virgin olive oil

1 clove garlic, peeled

1 small onion, thinly sliced

1 fresh rosemary sprig

1 fresh thyme sprig

6 fresh basil leaves

3 to 4 Italian plum tomatoes,
peeled, seeded, and coarsely chopped

2 pounds potatoes,
peeled and coarsely chopped

salt and pepper

2 teaspoons chopped parsley

Heat the olive oil in a heavy saucepan or deep skillet over medium heat. Add the garlic, onion, rosemary, and thyme. Sauté until the onions have softened, 4 to 5 minutes.

Add the basil, tomatoes, potatoes, salt, and pepper. Pour enough water over the potatoes to barely cover them.

Bring to a boil; immediately reduce the heat to a slow boil. Cook, uncovered, stirring occasionally, until the potatoes are cooked through and the liquid has reduced to a sauce consistency, about 20 minutes. If the sauce is too liquid, remove the potatoes with a slotted spoon to a casserole. Cover to keep warm. Boil the liquid until it has thickened slightly.

Pour the sauce over the potatoes, sprinkle with parsley and serve.

*10 SERVINGS*

12 fresh medium-sized artichokes

juice of 1 lemon

2 pounds baking potatoes

extra-virgin olive oil

dried bread crumbs

3 ounces grated Parmesan cheese

2 cloves garlic, peeled and thinly sliced

salt and pepper

## LA TORTIERA DI CARCIOFI E PATATE
### BAKED POTATO AND ARTICHOKE PIE

Clean the artichokes by removing the tough outside leaves and center. Cut into thin slices lengthwise and immediately put into cold water with the lemon juice.

Peel the potatoes and cut into 1/2-inch-thick slices.

Preheat the oven to 375°F.

Generously rub olive oil over the bottom and sides of a rectangular baking dish, approximately 9 by 12 inches, and sprinkle lightly with bread crumbs.

Line the dish with a layer of well-drained and dried artichokes. Sprinkle with Parmesan cheese, add third of the slices of garlic and drizzle lightly with olive oil.

Arrange a layer of potatoes over the artichokes. Dress with salt, pepper, and olive oil. Repeat the same sequence of ingredients, making two more layers. Sprinkle bread crumbs lightly on top and drizzle with olive oil.

Bake in the oven for about 40 minutes. Let rest 10 minutes before serving.

## CIPOLLINE ALLA CONTADINA
### COUNTRY-STYLE PEARL ONIONS

Put all ingredients, except the grapes, into a saucepan. Cover and simmer for 30 minutes over low heat, stirring occasionally.

Wash the grapes and stir into the onions. Cover and cook for about 20 minutes more or until done.

When cooked, let rest for about half an hour before serving. They are very good served at room temperature.

You can substitute golden raisins for the grapes.

*6 SERVINGS*

2 pounds small white pearl onions, peeled

2 tablespoons extra-virgin olive oil

1 ounce honey

1 teaspoon salt

pinch of pepper

1/2 pound each red and
white seedless grapes

## SEDANI STUFATI ALLA TOSCANA
### TUSCAN-STYLE STEWED CELERY

*6 SERVINGS*

2 large whole celery heads

2 tablespoons extra-virgin olive oil

1 small onion, finely chopped

1/4 cup dry white wine

7 ounces canned plum tomatoes, chopped

1 1/2 teaspoons salt

pinch of pepper

1/4 cup water

1 tablespoon parsley, chopped

Remove the toughest and greenest outer part of celery stalks and cut off the top leaves.

Remove the middle stalks and, using a small knife or potato peeler, remove the tough strings. The inside heart stalks don't need this care.

Wash the stalks and cut them into short pieces about 1 1/2 inches long. The widest stalks will need to be cut in half lengthwise before cutting into 1 1/2-inch-pieces.

Put the olive oil into a large saucepan. Add the onion. Cook over low heat until translucent. Pour in the white wine and let it evaporate slightly. Mix in the tomatoes, the celery pieces, salt, pepper, and water. Cover the pan and cook over low heat for about 50 minutes. Let rest about 15 minutes. Sprinkle with chopped parsley before serving.

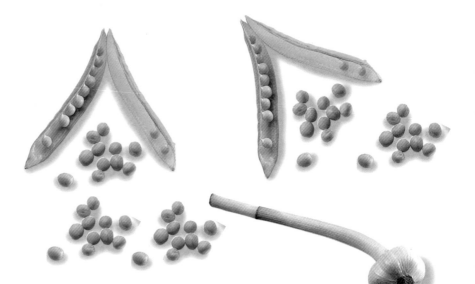

## PISELLI FRESCHI ALLA FIORENTINA
### FRESH PEAS ALLA FIORENTINA

Combine all of the ingredients, except the parsley, in a casserole and cook over high heat until it boils.

Lower the heat and cook for about 15 minutes. Discard garlic, sprinkle with parsley, and serve.

*6 SERVINGS*

1 pound fresh shelled peas

3 1/2 ounces prosciutto, diced

2 garlic cloves

3 tablespoons extra-virgin olive oil

1/2 cup boiling water

pinch of baking soda

1 teaspoon sugar

salt and pepper

1 tablespoon chopped parsley

## 8 SERVINGS

1 pound baby zucchini

3 tablespoons extra-virgin olive oil

2 cloves garlic

salt and pepper

1/3 cup vegetable broth

1 1/2 pounds carrots

1 ounce unsalted butter

1 teaspoon sugar

9 ounces frozen puff pastry, thawed

1 ounce fontina, thinly sliced

2 ounces Gruyère, coarsely grated

2 ounces Gorgonzola, separated into bits

2 tablespoons grated Parmesan cheese

1 egg yolk

# STRUDEL DI CAROTE E ZUCCHINE
## CARROT AND ZUCCHINI PIE

Wash the zucchini, dry, and cut into thin round slices.

In a large nonstick frying pan, heat the oil with one clove of garlic. Add the zucchini, season with salt and pepper, stir well, and cook for about 5 minutes. Add the broth, cover the pan, lower the heat, and cook for about 10 minutes more, until the broth has evaporated and the zucchini are soft. Let cool.

Peel the carrots, wash, dry and cut into thin round slices. Put the carrots into a heavy saucepan with butter, clove of garlic, salt, pepper, sugar, and 1/2 cup of water. Cook over medium heat, covered, until the carrots are tender. Remove from heat and let cool.

Preheat the oven to 375° F.

Roll out the puff pastry dough quite thin on a floured pastry board into a 10 by 15-inch rectangle.

Line a baking sheet with parchment paper. Place rolled-out pastry on it.

Cover the central part of it (about 3 by 6 inches) with a layer of fontina, put on top half of the carrots, and sprinkle with half of Gruyère and Gorgonzola.

Cover the cheeses with the zucchini, and sprinkle on top with the remaining Gruyère and Gorgonzola.

End with the remaining half of carrots and sprinkle with Parmesan cheese.

Fold the dough over the filling and seal well. Brush with egg yolk.

Bake in the oven for 45 minutes or until golden brown.

Remove from oven, transfer to a serving dish, and serve hot, cut into slices.

*8 SERVINGS*

2 pounds small zucchini

2 cups extra-virgin olive oil·

butter for greasing dish

salt and pepper

5 ounces Gorgonzola or blue cheese

2 teaspoons finely chopped parsley

2 large eggs

6 ounces sour cream

2 tablespoons grated Parmesan cheese

## ZUCCHINE AL GORGONZOLA
### ZUCCHINI WITH GORGONZOLA

Preheat the oven to 375°F.

Cut the zucchini into 1/4-inch-thick round slices.

Heat the oil in a large frying pan. Lightly fry the zucchini, a few at a time. Place the fried zucchini on paper towels to drain. Put the zucchini into a lightly greased baking dish. Season with salt and pepper.

In a small mixing bowl, mash the Gorgonzola cheese with a fork, add the finely chopped parsley, eggs, sour cream, Parmesan cheese, and a little salt and pepper.

Mix together well and pour over the zucchini.

Bake in the oven for 20 to 25 minutes.

**6** *SERVINGS*

12 small artichokes

juice of 1 lemon

7 ounces ricotta

2 ounces prosciutto

5 basil leaves

1 ounce fresh bread crumbs

1 large egg

salt and pepper

1/4 cup extra-virgin olive oil

1/2 cup dry white wine

1/2 cup water

# CARCIOFI RIPIENI CON RICOTTA
## ARTICHOKES STUFFED WITH RICOTTA

Preheat the oven to 375° F.

Clean the artichokes, removing the outer and center tough leaves. Put into a bowl with cool water and lemon juice.

Process the ricotta, prosciutto, basil, and bread crumbs in a food processor.

Add the egg to the mixture and combine well. Season with salt and pepper.

Stuff the artichokes with equal amounts of the filling.

Arrange the stuffed artichokes snugly together in an ovenproof casserole dish. Pour the oil, wine, and water into the dish. Cover the dish with parchment paper and close with a lid.

Cook in the oven for 30 minutes.

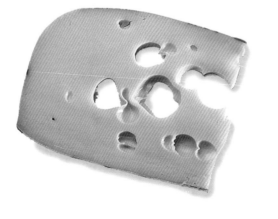

## PICCOLI SOUFFLÉ AGLI SPINACI E GROVIERA
SMALL SPINACH AND GRUYÈRE SOUFFLÉS

### 8 SERVINGS

2 pounds fresh spinach, washed

1 ounce unsalted butter,
plus extra for greasing molds

1 ounce all-purpose flour

1 cup boiling milk

salt and pepper

nutmeg

4 large eggs, separated

7 ounces Gruyère cheese, diced

2 tablespoons grated Parmesan cheese

dried bread crumbs

Preheat the oven to 375° F.

Boil the spinach and drain. Squeeze out the excess water and finely chop the spinach.

Melt the butter in a small saucepan. Stir in the flour, then slowly add the hot milk. Constantly stirring, cook the béchamel for 5 minutes. Season with salt and pepper. Take off the heat.

Add the spinach to the béchamel sauce and sprinkle with a little grated nutmeg. Let it cool.

Add the egg yolks, Gruyère, and the grated Parmesan cheese to the mixture.

Beat the egg whites until stiff. Gently fold into the mixture.

Grease 8 individual soufflé molds and dust with bread crumbs. Turn equal amounts of the mixture into each mold. Bake in the oven for 20 minutes.

Serve immediately.

## SPINACI CON UVETTA E PINOLI
### SPINACH WITH RAISINS AND PINE NUTS

Clean the spinach and wash well under cool running water.

Bring 2 quarts of water to a boil. When boiling, season with salt, add the spinach and cook until tender.

Drain the spinach and squeeze out excess water.

Melt the butter in a large skillet. Add the spinach and cook over medium heat for about 5 minutes. Season with salt and pepper. Stir in raisins and pine nuts and cook for another 5 minutes.

*6 SERVINGS*

2 pounds fresh spinach

salt and pepper

2 1/2 ounces unsalted butter

2 ounces golden raisins,
soaked in water for 10 minutes and drained

2 ounces pine nuts

## FAGIOLINI AL FORMAGGIO
### GREEN BEANS WITH CHEESE

Cut the ends off the green beans. Boil them in lightly salted water. Drain when still crisp.

Meantime, heat the oil in a frying pan, add the garlic and brown it gently. Add the anchovies and cook over medium heat, crushing them with a fork until very soft and almost dissolved.

Place the drained green beans into the skillet and toss. Cook for a minute or two over low heat. Season with pepper.

Beat the egg yolks and add the cream and cheese. Combine with the green beans and cook over medium heat, stirring frequently, for another 5 minutes. Serve hot.

*6 SERVINGS*

1 1/2 pounds fresh green beans

salt and pepper

1/4 cup extra-virgin olive oil

1 clove garlic

4 anchovy fillets, chopped

2 egg yolks

2 tablespoons heavy cream

3 ounces Certosa cheese
(or other soft, mild cheese, such as
cream cheese)

## PURÈ DI SEDANO RAPA
### MASHED CELERY ROOT

Cut the vegetables into 1-inch pieces.

Bring the milk to a boil in a saucepan and add the celery root and potatoes. Season with salt. Bring milk back to a boil, then immediately lower the heat. Simmer for 20 minutes until tender.

Transfer the vegetables to a food processor with a slotted spoon, reserving the milk.

Add a tablespoon or two of the reserved milk and blend until the vegetables become a thick, creamy consistency. If too thick, add a little more milk and process again.

Put the puréed vegetables into a heavy-bottomed saucepan and add the butter, Parmesan cheese, and a good pinch of nutmeg. Over low heat, stir the mixture with a wooden spoon until the butter is completely incorporated. Taste for seasoning.

Serve immediately or keep warm in the top pan of a double boiler over very low simmering water in the lower pan.

*6 SERVINGS*

1 1/2 pounds celery root, peeled

3/4 pound potatoes, peeled

1 quart milk

salt

1 ounce unsalted butter

1 ounce grated Parmesan cheese

grated nutmeg

*6 SERVINGS*

1 1/2 pounds medium-sized eggplants

1/2 clove garlic

1 teaspoon paprika

pinch of cayenne pepper (optional)

juice of 1/2 lemon

3 tablespoons extra-virgin olive oil

salt

7 ounces plain yogurt

1 tablespoon chopped parsley

# PURÈ DI MELANZANE
## EGGPLANT PURÉE

Preheat the oven to 400°F.

Wash the eggplants and pat them dry. Put on a baking sheet and cook in the oven until the skin is scorched and the inside is soft.

Remove and set aside to cool.

Remove the skins. Put the eggplant pulp into a blender with the garlic, paprika, cayenne pepper (if used), lemon juice, oil, and salt to taste.

Blend until the mixture becomes foamy.

Turn into a serving bowl. Add the yogurt and parsley and combine well.

## LA MIA RATATOUILLE
### MY RATATOUILLE

*6 SERVINGS*

1 1/2 pounds small zucchini

10 ounces eggplant

3 tablespoons extra-virgin olive oil

2 medium-sized onions, thinly sliced

2 cloves garlic, minced

1 red bell pepper, seeded, cored,
and cut into small pieces

1/2 teaspoon dried thyme

5 medium-sized ripe tomatoes,
seeded and diced

salt and pepper

1 tablespoon freshly chopped basil

Cut the zucchini and eggplant into 1/2-inch cubes.

Heat the olive oil in a large saucepan and sauté the onion with the garlic for a few minutes, stirring often.

Stir in the red pepper and cook over medium heat for 5 minutes.

Add the zucchini and eggplant, combine well, and simmer briefly. Add a little hot water when the vegetables begin sticking to the bottom of the pan.

Stir in the thyme and tomatoes. Season to taste with salt and pepper. Cook over low heat for about 25 minutes, stirring frequently.

Just before serving, stir in the basil.

## MELANZANE IN SAOR
### SWEET AND SOUR EGGPLANT

Cut the eggplants into very thin slices, crosswise.

Salt the slices and let rest for about 1 hour in a colander until they lose their bitter liquid.

Pat dry. Heat the oil and fry the eggplant slices a few at a time. As slices are browned and cooked, remove with a slotted spoon and drain on paper towels.

Season with salt and pepper.

Prepare the following marinade:
Heat 1/2 cup of olive oil and sauté the onions and garlic in a saucepan for 2 minutes. Add the vinegar, pine nuts, golden raisins, and parsley. Cook for 15 minutes over low heat.

Arrange the eggplant slices in a shallow bowl. Cover with the marinade.

Cool to room temperature. Cover and refrigerate for 1 day before serving.

*8 TO 10 SERVINGS*

3 pounds medium-sized eggplants

2 cups extra-virgin olive oil

salt and pepper

1/2 cup extra-virgin olive oil for marinating

3 medium-sized onions, thinly sliced

1 clove garlic, chopped

1 cup white wine vinegar

1 ounce pine nuts

1 ounce golden raisins

1 small bunch of parsley, finely chopped

## GRAN MISTO FREDDO
### COLD MIXED VEGETABLES

*6 TO 8 SERVINGS*

3/4 pound medium-sized eggplants

3/4 pound baby zucchini

salt and pepper

1/3 pound mushrooms

1/4 cup extra-virgin olive oil

1 small onion, thinly sliced

1 small celery stalk, chopped

1 clove garlic, chopped

3 tablespoons white wine vinegar

1 tablespoon capers

1 tablespoon sugar

2 large tomatoes, chopped

2 ounces black olives, pitted

Cut the eggplant and the zucchini into small cubes and sprinkle with salt. Let them drain in a colander for 1/2 hour. Rinse and pat dry.

Clean the mushrooms and slice into 1/4-inch-thick slices.

Heat the oil in a large casserole, add the eggplant, zucchini, mushrooms, onion, celery, and garlic.

Cook for 10 minutes over medium-high heat, stirring frequently. Add the vinegar, capers, sugar, salt, and pepper to taste. Mix gently and lower the heat. Cover and let simmer for 10 to 15 minutes. Add the tomatoes and olives. Bring to a boil for a few minutes. Remove from heat and turn into a bowl.

Let cool to room temperature. Refrigerate for a couple of hours before serving.

*8 SERVINGS*

6 ounces lean bacon or lean salt pork, diced

extra-virgin olive oil

6 ounces sliced Emmenthal cheese

1 pound fresh spinach, washed and dried, large leaves cut in half

3 kiwis, peeled and thinly sliced

1 tablespoon pine nuts

salt

juice of 1/2 lemon

# INSALATA DI KIWI
## KIWI SALAD

Lightly brown the bacon in a little olive oil.

Cut the cheese into strips.

Put the spinach, kiwi, bacon, Emmenthal cheese, and pine nuts into a salad bowl. Dress with oil, salt, and lemon juice.

Gently combine and let sit for 10 minutes before serving.

# SUGGESTED WINES

Vin Santo del Chianti **Ruffino**

Malvasia delle Lipari

Picolit del Collio

Recioto di Valpolicella

Brachetto d'Acqui

Ramandolo dei Colli Orientali del Friuli

# Desserts

# SEMIFREDDO AL CAFFÈ DI ANGELICA
## ANGELICA'S BAVARIAN DESSERT

Line a rectangular 9 by 4-inch mold or loaf pan with a sheet of plastic wrap, sticking it evenly to all sides.

Soften the gelatin in 1/4 cup of cool water. Place in double boiler and dissolve. Stir in the instant coffee.

Coarsely chop the Torrone, chocolate, and hazelnuts. Crumble the cookies. Combine these ingredients well. Set aside.

Beat the egg yolks and the sugar with an electric beater. Add the mascarpone and the gelatin with coffee. Beat briefly until combined well.

Beat the egg whites until stiff.

Whip the heavy cream.

Fold the whipped cream into the coffee mixture with a rubber spatula, then fold in the egg whites.

Put half the Torrone, chocolate, hazelnuts, and cookie mixture into the lined mold.

Pour the coffee cream over it and cover with the remaining Torrone mixture.

Cover the surface with plastic wrap and freeze.

Remove from freezer two hours before serving, and place in the lowest part of the refrigerator.

Unmold and serve sliced.

\* Nougat with nuts, available in Italian specialty stores.

*8 TO 10 SERVINGS*

1 envelope plain gelatin

1 tablespoon instant coffee

5 ounces Torrone \*

5 ounces bittersweet chocolate

20 roasted hazelnuts

5 butter cookies

3 egg yolks

6 tablespoons sugar

8 ounces mascarpone

2 egg whites

1 cup heavy cream

## SPUMA ALLO YOGURT
### BAVARIAN YOGURT CAKE

Line a 5-cup plum cake mold with a sheet of plastic wrap, sticking it to all sides evenly.

Soften gelatin in 1/4 cup of cold water, and melt in a double boiler.

With an electric beater, whip the egg yolks with 1/4 cup sugar until they are nearly white. Fold in the vanilla and yogurt with a rubber spatula. Add the melted gelatin and mix well.

Whip the cream and fold it into the mixture.

Whip the egg whites until stiff. Whip in 1 tablespoon of sugar. Fold the egg whites into the yogurt mixture.

Pour the batter into the mold.

Brush one side of the ladyfingers with the combined orange juice and Grand Marnier. Lay the cookies side by side over the top, brushed side down, onto the cream. Gently push the cookies into the mixture.

Cover the mold with plastic wrap and freeze for 1 hour. Remove and put in the refrigerator for 2 hours before unmolding the cake.

Cover the bottom of dessert plates with apricot sauce (see following recipe,). Cut the Bavarian cake into slices and place one slice over the sauce on each plate.

*8 TO 10 SERVINGS*

1 envelope plain gelatin

2 large eggs, separated

1/4 cup sugar, plus 1 tablespoon

1 teaspoon vanilla extract

2 cups plain yogurt

1 cup heavy cream

12 ladyfingers

freshly squeezed juice of 1 orange

1 tablespoon Grand Marnier liqueur

## SALSA DI ALBICOCCHE
### APRICOT SAUCE

Combine the jam, orange juice, and liqueur in a saucepan.

Slowly melt the ingredients together over low heat. As soon as the ingredients are mixed together well, add the candied orange rinds, remove from heat and let it cool.

*8 SERVINGS*

1 1/2 cups apricot jam

juice of 2 oranges, strained

3 tablespoons Grand Marnier

3 1/2 ounces candied orange rinds, thinly sliced

## MACEDONIA IN TORTA
### FRUIT SALAD CAKE

*8 TO 10 SERVINGS*

1 banana
2 apples
2 slices fresh pineapple
1 pear
1 peach
1 tablespoon pine nuts
1 tablespoon golden raisins
2 tablespoons apricot jam
2 tablespoons brandy
2 tablespoons dry white wine
5 ounces unsalted butter,
plus extra for greasing pan
1 1/2 cups sifted all-purpose flour,
plus extra for dusting pan
4 large eggs, separated
5 ounces sugar
1 envelope dry yeast
grated zest of 1 lemon
confectioners' sugar

Peel all of the fruit and cut it into bite-sized cubes. Place in a large bowl and add the pine nuts and raisins.

Mix the fruit with the jam, brandy, and white wine and set aside.

Preheat the oven to 350°F.

Melt the butter over low heat without letting it turn brown.

Mix the flour with the melted butter, egg yolks, sugar, yeast, and lemon zest together in a large bowl. The dough should be semihard.

Add the fruit salad and mix very well. Whip the egg whites to a fine creamy texture and fold them into the fruit salad mixture.

Grease and dust the inside of a round 9-inch springform pan. Pour the mixture into it and cook in the oven for approximately 30 minutes. Cover the cake with foil and cook for another 30 minutes.

Dust with sifted confectioners' sugar before serving.

The cake can be served cold or warm.

## CROSTATA AL LIMONE
### LEMON TART

*8 SERVINGS*

FOR THE DOUGH:
2 cups all-purpose flour
1 cup sugar
1 cup unsalted butter
1 large egg
grated zest of 1 lemon

FOR THE FILLING:
1 cup egg whites
1 cup sugar
1/2 cup lemon juice

Preheat the oven to 350°F.

To make the dough:
Quickly knead together the flour, sugar, butter, egg, and lemon zest.

Smooth out the dough in a round 9-inch springform pan with fingertips. Prick the bottom with a fork.

Bake in the oven for approximately 15 minutes, until the pastry is slightly hardened but not cooked. Remove from the oven.

To make the filling:
Beat the egg whites and the sugar with a whisk for 30 seconds.

Add the lemon juice and combine well.

Pour the filling into the pan lined with the pastry.

Bake in the oven for 30 to 40 minutes. Cover with foil after the first 5 minutes to keep the surface of the cake white.

*8 TO 10 SERVINGS*

16 ounces canned pear halves in syrup, drained and sliced

FOR THE PASTRY:

2 cups all-purpose flour

1 cup unsalted butter

1 cup sugar

1 large egg

grated zest of 1 lemon

FOR THE CUSTARD:

2 egg yolks

1/2 cup sugar

1 teaspoon vanilla extract

2 tablespoons sifted cornstarch

1 cup sour cream

1/2 cup heavy cream

# TORTA DI PERE SCIROPPATE
## PEAR PIE

Preheat the oven to 350°F.

To make the pastry:
Quickly knead all the ingredients together. Spread the dough onto a round 9-inch springform pan. Prick the bottom of the dough with a fork.

Cook in the oven for approximately 15 minutes, until the pastry is slightly hardened.

Remove from the oven and cover the pastry with the drained and sliced pears.

To make the custard:
Mix the egg yolks with the sugar and vanilla in a small saucepan.

Stir in the cornstarch and the sour cream and cook on a low heat until it thickens, about 10 minutes.

Cool slightly and stir in the heavy cream.

Pour the custard into the pastry shell and bake in the oven for another 40 minutes. Cover with foil when the surface starts to brown.

*8 TO 10 SERVINGS*

FOR THE PASTRY:

1 1/4 cups all-purpose flour

1/3 cup cornstarch

1 cup sugar

1 cup unsalted butter

1 egg

pinch of cinnamon

FOR THE CUSTARD:

2 eggs

1/2 cup sugar

1 ounce sifted all-purpose flour

2 cups milk

FOR THE FILLING:

10 ounces ricotta

2 egg yolks

1/4 cup heavy cream

grated zest of 1 lemon

2 tablespoons golden raisins,
soaked in 1/2 cup of Vin Santo
(Italian sweet wine)

# TORTA DI RICOTTA
## RICOTTA CAKE

Preheat the oven to 375°F.

To make the pastry:
Quickly knead together all the ingredients. Smooth out the dough evenly, lining a round 9-inch springform pan. Cool in the refrigerator.

To make the custard:
Beat the eggs with the sugar in a saucepan with a heavy bottom. Add the flour. Bring the milk to a boil and stir into eggs and sugar mixture. Cook over very low heat, continuously stirring, until the liquid thickens (about 10 minutes). Let the cream rest until lukewarm, stirring occasionally.

To make the filling:
Pass the ricotta through a sieve or food mill and add to the custard cream along with the egg yolks, heavy cream, lemon zest, and golden raisins.

Pour the mixture into the pan lined with the cooled pastry.

Cook in the oven for 45 minutes. Cover with foil when surface starts to brown.

## TORTA DI CAROTE
### CARROT CAKE

*8 SERVINGS*

10 ounces carrots

3 1/2 ounces ground blanched, skinned almonds

1 ounce amaretti cookies

4 large eggs, separated

1/3 cup sugar

grated zest of 1 lemon

1 ounce sifted cornstarch

1/2 teaspoon dry yeast

salt

butter and dried bread crumbs for the mold

confectioners' sugar

Preheat the oven to 375° F.

Peel and finely grate the carrots. Pat dry in a clean dish cloth.

Process the almonds to a fine consistency. Crumble the amaretti cookies.

Beat the egg yolks with the sugar with an electric beater. Add the grated lemon zest. Add the cornstarch, yeast and a pinch of salt.

Stir in the carrots, almonds, and amaretti, with a rubber spatula and combine well.

Beat the egg whites. Gently fold into the mixture, little by little.

Grease a round 9-inch springform pan and dust with bread crumbs. Pour the batter into it.

Cook in the oven for 45 minutes. Cover the cake with foil after the first 15 minutes.

Dust with sifted confectioners' sugar before serving.

## TORTA ALLE ALBICOCCHE
### APRICOT CAKE

Preheat the oven to 375° F.

Line a round 9-inch cake pan with parchment paper. Roll out the pastry and cut it into a 10-inch circle. Fit the puff pastry in the pan. Prick bottom in several places with a fork and place the apricot halves on it, cut sides down, completely covering the pastry. Sprinkle with 1 tablespoon of sugar.

Bake in the oven for 15 minutes.

Meantime, gently beat the eggs with the remaining sugar and vanilla. Dissolve the cornstarch in the cream. Add the yogurt and pour this mixture into the egg and sugar batter.

Remove the pan from the oven and press the pastry down with fingertips if it puffed up during cooking.

Pour in the batter and return to the oven for 40 minutes, covering the cake after 10 minutes with foil.

Remove from oven and cool. Dust with sifted confectioners' sugar before serving.

*6 SERVINGS*

1/2 pound frozen puff pastry, thawed

1 1/2 pounds ripe fresh apricots,
cut in half, pitted

1/4 cup sugar

2 large eggs

1 teaspoon vanilla extract

2 teaspoons cornstarch

3/4 cup heavy cream

1/2 cup plain yogurt

confectioners' sugar for dusting

# TORTA ROVESCIATA ALL'ANANAS
## PINEAPPLE UPSIDE-DOWN CAKE

Preheat the oven to 350° F.

Grease a round nonstick 8-inch cake pan.

In a medium-sized saucepan, over low heat, combine 1/2 cup of the sugar and 1/4 cup of butter, stirring until well combined and smooth.

Remove from heat and pour into the bottom of the cake pan.

Cover with the fresh pineapple.

Sift flour and mix with baking soda, baking powder, and a pinch of salt.

Beat the remaining butter (1/4 cup) with the remaining sugar (3/4 cup) until smooth. Add vanilla. Beat in the eggs, one at a time. Mix well. Stir in flour mixture and fold in the sour cream. Stir well and pour into the pan over the pineapple.

Bake in the oven for 40 to 50 minutes, covering with foil if the surface begins to brown.

Allow to stand 5 minutes in pan before inverting onto a round serving dish. Don't remove pan until the cake has cooled.

*6 TO 8 SERVINGS*

1/2 cup unsalted butter,
plus extra for greasing pan

1 1/4 cups brown sugar

1 small fresh ripe pineapple, peeled, cored,
and coarsely chopped

3 ounces all-purpose flour

1/2 teaspoon baking soda

1/2 teaspoon baking powder

salt

1/2 teaspoon vanilla extract

2 large eggs

1/4 cup sour cream

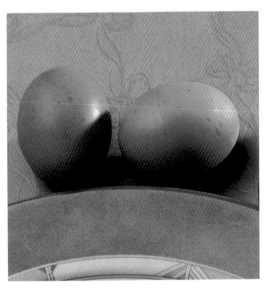

# TORTA DI MELE
## APPLE CAKE

Preheat the oven to 350°F.

Beat the eggs with half of the sugar. Add half of the melted butter.

Add flour, yeast, milk, lemon zest, and a pinch of salt.

Peel the apples and thinly slice them. Reserve two apples to cover the top of the cake. Put the sliced apples into the egg mixture and combine well.

Grease and flour a round 8-inch springform cake pan and pour the mixture into it. Cover the top with the slices of the two reserved apples. Pour the remaining melted butter over the top. Sprinkle evenly with the remaining sugar. Cover the top with foil.

Bake in the oven for 45 minutes. Remove the foil for the last 10 minutes of cooking.

Let cool and unmold.

*6 SERVINGS*

3 large eggs

3/4 cup sugar

1/3 cup unsalted melted butter,
plus extra for greasing pan

1 1/2 cups sifted all-purpose flour

1 teaspoon dry yeast

1 cup milk

grated zest of 1 lemon

salt

3 pounds Delicious apples

# STRUDEL

Preheat the oven to 350°F.

Peel the apples and the pears and cut into thin slices. Gently toss in 1/2 cup of sugar.

Melt 3 ounces of the butter in a little pan over moderate heat, add the bread crumbs and toast for a few minutes. Set aside to cool.

Roll out the puff pastry very thin on a floured pastry board.

Line a baking sheet with parchment paper and place the pastry on it.

Cover the center of the pastry with toasted bread crumbs, then with a layer of sliced apples and pears, raisins, pine nuts, cinnamon, and lemon zest. Continue alternating the ingredients until used.

Carefully fold the pastry, sealing it well.

Melt the remaining butter. Brush the surface of the strudel with it, and sprinkle with the remaining tablespoon of sugar.

Cook for about 1 hour, sprinkling the surface from time to time with cooking juice.

Remove from oven. Transfer to a serving plate and cool. Sprinkle with sifted confectioners' sugar before serving.

*10 SERVINGS*

2 pounds green apples

1 pound fresh pears

1/2 cup sugar, plus 1 tablespoon

4 ounces unsalted butter

3 tablespoons dried bread crumbs

14 ounces frozen puff pastry, thawed

flour for pastry board

10 ounces golden raisins, soaked in 1/4 cup of brandy for 10 minutes, drained

3 ounces pine nuts

1 teaspoon ground cinnamon

finely grated zest of 1 lemon

confectioners' sugar

# BUDINO NERO
## BLACK PUDDING

Preheat the oven to 325°F.

Put 3 tablespoons of sugar in a small saucepan with enough water to completely dampen the sugar. Put on low heat and cook until the sugar becomes golden brown. Pour it immediately into a rectangular mold with a 4-cup capacity. Turn it quickly to allow the sugar to cover bottom and sides.

Place the milk, chocolate, and chopped ladyfingers in a saucepan over low heat, bring to a boil, and continue to cook for 1 to 2 minutes.

Beat the eggs with the sugar, vanilla, and a pinch of salt with an electric beater.

Add the milk, chocolate, and ladyfinger mixture to the egg and sugar mixture and beat together briefly.

Pour the mixture into the caramelized mold and cook in a covered bain-marie in the oven for 1 1/2 hours or more until firm.

Remove from the bain-marie and cool.

Refrigerate the pudding overnight before serving.

Just before serving, unmold the pudding. Cut it into slices and serve with a kiwi sauce. To make kiwi sauce:
Process 2 peeled and chopped kiwi fruits with 2 teaspoons of sugar and 1/2 cup of heavy cream for few seconds in the food processor.

*8 SERVINGS*

3 tablespoons sugar,
to caramelize the mold

3 cups milk

5 ounces bittersweet chocolate

12 ladyfingers, coarsely chopped

4 large eggs

1/2 cup sugar

1/2 teaspoon vanilla extract

salt

*4 SERVINGS*

4 stale brioche rolls

2 ounces golden raisins

grated zest of half a lemon

3 large eggs

1/2 cup sugar

2 cups milk

confectioners' sugar

# BUDINO DEI MEDICI
## MEDICEAN PUDDING

Preheat the oven to 375°F.

Cut each brioche in 1/3-inch-thick slices, crosswise, and fit them snugly into a shallow baking pan.

Sprinkle with the raisins and the lemon zest over the top.

Beat the eggs with sugar until well combined.

Bring the milk to a boil, add the hot milk to the eggs, stir well, and immediately pour over the brioches, pressing them gently so they absorb the liquid.

Place the pudding immediately in the oven and cook for 20 minutes. Take out from the oven and cool.

Just before serving, dust with sifted confectioners' sugar.

Recipe is easily doubled. Cook for 30 minutes.

# CREMA ALLE PESCHE CON MASCARPONE E AMARETTI
## PEACH CREAM WITH MASCARPONE AND AMARETTI

Beat the egg whites until stiff.

Whip cream until it peaks.

Beat the egg yolks with the sugar until nearly white. Add the mascarpone and mix well. (Use an electric hand mixer for these four operations.)

With a rubber spatula, fold the Cognac into the mixture. Then gently fold in the whipped cream and the beaten egg whites.

Cut the peaches into little cubes and add to mixture. Crumble the amaretti cookies and gently stir into the mascarpone mixture.

Pour the peach cream into a serving bowl and refrigerate for at least 2 to 3 hours before serving.

If available, instead of canned, use peeled and pitted ripe fresh peaches, sliced very thin.

*10 SERVINGS*

2 egg whites

8 ounces heavy cream

3 egg yolks

6 tablespoons sugar

8 ounces mascarpone

2 tablespoons Cognac

1 1/4 pounds canned peach halves, drained

2 ounces amaretti cookies

## MOUSSE DI CIOCCOLATO
### CHOCOLATE MOUSSE

*8 SERVINGS*

7 ounces bittersweet chocolate

1 cup bitter espresso coffee

2 large eggs, separated

1 cup heavy cream

2 tablespoons sugar

Melt the chocolate and the coffee in a double boiler.

Separately, with an electric beater, beat the egg whites until stiff, the cream until it peaks, and the egg yolks with the sugar until nearly white.

Add the melted chocolate to the egg yolks and sugar, and mix quickly with an electric beater.

With a rubber spatula, fold in the whipped cream, then the egg whites.

Pour the mixture in a crystal serving bowl, cover it with plastic wrap, and refrigerate overnight before serving.

## BAVARESE AL CAFFÈ
## CON SALSA DI CIOCCOLATO
BAVARIAN COFFEE PUDDING WITH CHOCOLATE SAUCE

*8 TO 10 SERVINGS*

FOR THE PUDDING:

3 egg yolks

1/2 cup sugar

1 1/4 cups milk

1 envelope plain gelatin

1/2 cup espresso coffee

1 cup heavy cream

FOR THE CHOCOLATE SAUCE:

7 ounces bittersweet chocolate

1 ounce unsalted butter

1/4 cup hot espresso coffee

In a heavy-bottomed saucepan beat the egg yolks with the sugar until white.

Bring the milk to a boil and, little by little, stir it into the egg mixture.

Put the saucepan over low heat and, constantly stirring, bring to a boil. Remove from heat and add the gelatin, previously soaked in 1/4 cup of cold water. Add the espresso coffee and set aside to cool.

Whip cream until it peaks. Little by little, add the coffee mixture to the whipped cream.

Line a 9 by 4-inch rectangular mold or loaf pan with plastic wrap and pour the mixture into it.

Refrigerate for several hours until it is completely chilled.

Invert onto a serving dish and unmold.

To make the chocolate sauce:
Melt the chocolate in a double boiler with the butter. Add the hot espresso.
When the chocolate has melted, remove from heat and cool until lukewarm. If the sauce is too thick, add a little milk or cream.

# TORTA AL CIOCCOLATO
## CHOCOLATE CAKE

Preheat the oven to 375°F.

Melt the chocolate with the butter in a double boiler.

Beat the egg whites with an electric beater untill stiff.

Beat the egg yolks and confectioners' sugar until creamy. Add cornstarch.

When the chocolate has melted, add it to the egg yolks and sugar and mix it quickly with an electric beater.

Gently fold in the egg whites, stirring from bottom to top with a rubber spatula.

Butter a round 9-inch springform cake pan and dust with flour .

Turn the mixture into the pan. Cook in the oven for 20 minutes.

Let it cool before unmolding. Sprinkle the top with sifted confectioners' sugar before serving.

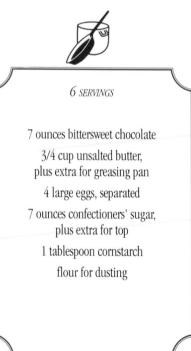

*6 SERVINGS*

7 ounces bittersweet chocolate

3/4 cup unsalted butter,
plus extra for greasing pan

4 large eggs, separated

7 ounces confectioners' sugar,
plus extra for top

1 tablespoon cornstarch

flour for dusting

# BAVARESE AI MARRONI
## BAVARIAN DESSERT WITH CHESTNUTS

Put the gelatin in a bowl with 1/4-cup cold water to soften.

Bring the milk to a boil with the vanilla.

Beat the egg yolks with the sugar together well in a bowl. Add the boiling milk, little by little, constantly mixing with a wooden spoon.

Turn the mixture into a saucepan with a heavy bottom and place over very low heat, stirring continuously, until it thickens (about 10 to 15 minutes). Don't let it come to a boil.

Remove from heat and add the gelatin and mix well. Add the chestnut jam and combine well.

Let it cool to lukewarm.

Whip the heavy cream. Gently fold it into the mixture.

Line the inside of a rectangular or round mold with plastic wrap. Pour the mixture into the mold, cover with plastic wrap, and refrigerate overnight.

Unmold the Bavarian dessert just before serving and decorate with sweetened whipped cream and crumbled candied chestnuts.

*8 SERVINGS*

1 envelope plain gelatin

3/4 cup milk

1 teaspoon vanilla extract

3 egg yolks

1/4 cup sugar

12 ounces chestnut preserves (Available in specialty food shops. There is no substitute.)

1 cup heavy cream

1 cup lightly sweetened whipped cream

4 candied chestnuts for decoration

**8 SERVINGS**

8 small oranges
3/4 cup sugar
3/4 cup water
Grand Marnier

# ARANCE LACCATE
## CANDIED ORANGES

Wash and dry the oranges. Peel 4 of them (just the zest part of the skin) and cut the skin into very thin pine needle shapes.

Put the sugar, the water, and the orange peels into a small saucepan. Put on a low heat and let it boil for about 20 minutes, stirring occasionally, until a thick syrup has formed.

Remove from heat and add 3 tablespoons of Grand Marnier.

While the orange peels are boiling, remove the outer skin from all oranges with a very sharp knife. Place the oranges in a serving bowl.

When the syrup is done, pour it over the oranges immediately. Top each orange with equal amounts of the candied orange pine needles.

Cool at room temperature for at least 20 minutes before serving.

# UVA BRINATA
## ICED GRAPES

Wash the grapes carefully and dry in a towel.

Divide the grapes into individual little bunches.

In a small bowl, beat the egg whites with a fork until smooth, but not foamy.

Dip the grapes into the egg whites.

Place a thick layer of granulated sugar on a plate and roll the bunches in it so that each grape is completely covered.

Place them on parchment paper and let them sit for a few hours before arranging on a serving dish.

The iced grapes are delicious to eat and also make a beautiful table garnish for elegant parties.

*4 SERVINGS*

1 pound white, red, or black table grapes
3 egg whites
granulated sugar

# INDEX

# ANTIPASTO AND SEAFOOD

# PASTA AND FIRST-COURSE DISHES

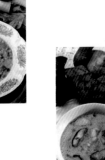

# MEAT

# VEGETABLE SIDE DISHES

# DESSERTS